916.49

TWINPACK
Gran Canaria

JACKIE STADDON AND HILARY WESTON

If you have any comments
or suggestions for this guide
you can contact the editor at
Twinpacks@theAA.com

AA Publishing
Find out more about AA Publishing and the wide
range of services the AA provides by visiting our
website at theAA.com/bookshop

How to Use This Book

KEY TO SYMBOLS

✚ Map reference

✉ Address

☎ Telephone number

🕐 Opening/closing times

🍴 Restaurant or café

🚌 Nearest bus route

⛴ Nearest ferry route

♿ Facilities for visitors with disabilities

❓ Other practical information

▷ Further information

ℹ Tourist information

✋ Admission charges: Expensive (over €9), Moderate (€3–€9), and Inexpensive (under €3)

★ Major sight   ★ Minor sight

👣 Walks   🚌 Drives

🏬 Shops

🎵 Entertainment and Activities

🍴 Restaurants

This guide is divided into four sections

• **Essential Gran Canaria:** An introduction to the island and tips on making the most of your stay.

• **Gran Canaria by Area:** We've broken the island into four areas, and recommended the best sights, shops, activities, restaurants, entertainment and nightlife venues in each one. Suggested walks and drives help you to explore.

• **Where to Stay:** The best hotels, whether you're looking for luxury, budget or something in between.

• **Need to Know:** The info you need to make your trip run smoothly, including getting about by public transport, weather tips, emergency phone numbers and useful websites.

Navigation In the Gran Canaria by Area chapter, we've given each area its own colour, which is also used on the locator maps throughout the book and the map on the inside front cover.

Maps The fold-out map accompanying this book is a comprehensive map of Gran Canaria. The grid on this fold-out map is the same as the grid on the locator maps within the book. The grid references to these maps are shown with capital letters, for example A1. The grid references to the town plan are shown with lower-case letters, for example a1.

Contents

Introducing Gran Canaria

For many, the image Gran Canaria conjures up is of sun, sand and booze. Dig deeper and you will soon discover a lot more: a small island race with a long history, dramatic coastlines, spectacular ravines, mountain views and pine forests.

This is not a large island—you can drive around it in a day—but its diverse geographical features and its ancient culture make it a fascinating place to visit. Closer to Africa than Europe, until the 1960s it was just a dot in the ocean, a convenient place for ships to refit and stock up. With the emergence of the package tour it soon became the ideal year-round holiday playground, with a perfect climate and only a few hours' flying time from mainland Europe.

The ensuing construction of the high-rise conurbations on the south coast may have been detrimental to the island's reputation, but not to its economy. It has taken several decades for the authorities to begin to promote the island for its rural tourism, its excellent golf courses and its more sophisticated resorts, such as Puerto Mogán and the expanding Meloneras. The brash worlds of Playa del Inglés and Puerto Rico still exist, but even here there are attempts to landscape and improve. Some of the *centros commerciales* in these resorts may look tired and tacky but new classier designs are emerging.

Gran Canaria may not be beautifully lush but it is dramatically diverse. The central region, with its volcanic craters and hillsides dotted with ancient caves, offers a majestic tranquillity. You can walk in delightful pine forests, take a boat trip to view the golden sands and craggy coastline from the water, uncover the history of the island with a trip to the capital, Las Palmas, and experience authentic Canarian life away from the major resorts.

Facts + Figures

● **Population: 800,000 of which 400,000 live in Las Palmas**
● **Around 2.5 million tourists visit Gran Canaria each year**
● **Total area: 1,532sq km (591sq miles)**
● **Highest point: Pozo de las Nieves 1,949m (6,392ft)**

STREET NAMES

Many street names in Las Palmas originate from famous Canarians, often with lengthy names, who are little known outside the island. You will encounter engineer Léon y Castillo; poets Nicolas Estévanez and Tomás Morales; historian and naturalist José Viera y Clavijo; collector of antiquities Dr.Chil; novelist Pérez Galdós and many more.

CANARIAN WRESTLING

This sport, known in Spanish as *lucha canaria*, has its roots in the pre-conquest days of the Guanche people. Originally a test of manhood, it is now a popular spectator sport with a fervent crowd cheering on the opponents. Two men enter the arena barefoot and after preliminary rituals of gentlemanly greeting they set out to try and unbalance the other by grabbing the hem of the opponent's shorts. No part of the body other than the feet may touch the ground, if it does that man loses.

DRAGON TREE

This distinctive looking tree (*Dracaena draco*) is one of the last survivors of the Ice Age. Its thick bare trunk grows to a height of around 12m (39ft) and is crowned by spiky green leaves. When its bark or leaves are cut it secretes a blood-red resin used by the early Guanche people for its medicinal and magical powers.

A Short Stay in Gran Canaria

DAY 1: LAS PALMAS

Morning Start your day early, in the old quarter at the **Vegueta market** (▷ 30), where you will get the chance to mingle with locals and admire the huge selection of produce for sale.

Mid-morning Stop for a coffee, tea or juice at the **Tea and Coffee Pot** (▷ 44) in Calle Mendizábal and watch the world go by. If you are interested in modern art, call in at **CAAM** (▷ 32) for the latest on the Canarian arts scene, then head for the **Museo Canario** (▷ 27) to learn about the earliest inhabitants of the island. From here you can see the imposing **Catedral de Santa Ana** (▷ 26). Walk round it to the **Casa de Colón** (▷ 24–25) where you can explore the history of Las Palmas and the exploits of Christopher Columbus.

Lunch There are several eating options in Vegueta; try **Casa Montesdeoca** (▷ 43) for an expensive but delightful choice or **El Herreño** (▷ 43) near the market for Canarian cooking or simple *tapas*.

Afternoon Leave Vegueta and cross the main road into Triana for some mainstream shopping. Alternatively take bus 1, 12 or 13 to Avenida Mesa y Lopéz for designer names. If you prefer to chill out on the beach, take the 1, 12, 13 or 41 up to **Playa de las Canteras** (▷ 29).

Dinner If you opt for the beach, try **La Marinera** (▷ 43) at the far end for great fish dishes and sea views. If you are staying in town **La Cava Triana** (▷ 43) is a good option for some Spanish cooking.

Evening To end the day, chance a flutter at the casino in **Hotel Santa Catalina** (▷ 40) or have a relaxing drink in **Terraza la Marina** (▷ 41) after an evening stroll along the promenade.

DAY 2: PUERTO RICO AND PUERTO DE MOGÁN

Morning Start your day from the bus terminal at **Puerto Rico** (▷ 60), and stroll down through the central gardens to the beachfront. Select one of the cafés along the promenade for a coffee stop from where you can watch the world go by. Either side of the beach boards advertise watersports—why not test your skills at windsurfing or paragliding?

Mid-morning Head right to Puerto Escala and take the steps to the top of the sea wall. From here take the clifftop path that leads to Amadores, an easy 1km (0.6 miles) walk away. Playa de los Amadores has a fine artifical beach and a developing resort climbing the cliffs behind. On a clear day, from here there are views across to Mount Teide on Tenerife.

Lunch Stay in Amadores for lunch. Palm Restaurant has a large terrace right on the beach and does good tapas and salads. After you've eaten take a gentle stroll back to Puerto Rico.

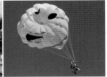

Afternoon When back in Puerto Rico, walk to the end of the harbour wall and jump aboard the glass-bottom boat over to **Puerto de Mogán** (▷ 56–57), the island's most charming resort. The journey takes about 15 minutes, and along the way you will pass steep cliffs and secluded bays. On your arrival in Puerto de Mogán spend an hour or two on the beach topping up your tan.

Dinner Head for the harbour before the sun goes down and take an early dinner at one of the excellent fish restaurants: **Restaurante Cofradia** (▷ 70) and **La Caracola** (▷ 68) are two of the best.

Evening After dinner explore the harbour area before stopping for a drink by the water while the sun sets behind the cliffs.

Top 25

► ► ►

Cenobio de Valerón

Santa María de Guía

Tamadaba
Hondo de Abajo

Andén Verde

Parque Nacional

Artenara

CENTRAL GRAN CANARIA 71–86
1415
Roque Bentaiga 1803
Roque Nublo

Parque Nacional

Puerto de Mogán

Palmitos Parque

Mu Abor

Maspalomas

Dunas Maspalon

These pages are a quick guide to the Top 25, which are described in more detail later. Here they are listed alphabetically, and the tinted background shows which area they are in.

Caldera de Bandama ▷ **90–91** Take a hike down the path that leads into the crater.

Casa de Colón, Las Palmas ▷ **24–25** Check out the city's history and the early explorers.

Catedral de Santa Ana, Las Palmas ▷ **26** ▼▼▼ Imposing cathedral comprising a mix of styles.

Cenobio de Valerón ▷ **92** One of the most important archaeological sites in Gran Canaria.

Dunas de Maspalomas ▷ **50–51** Saharan-like dunes that are a natural wonder.

Fataga ▷ **76–77** Pretty as a picture, this village is known for its apricot festival.

Fortaleza Grande ▷ **78** The final stronghold of the Guanches in their fight against the Spanish.

Jardín Botánico Canario ▷ **94–95** The largest botanic gardens in Spain.

Maspalomas ▷ **52** An upmarket resort with luxury hotels fronted by magnificent dunes.

Mundo Aborigen ▷ **53** Open-air museum bringing to life the story of the Guanche people.

Palmitos Parque ▷ **54** See animals, birds and plants in a wonderful natural setting.

Museo Elder, Las Palmas ▷ **28** Science and technology are made fun in this excellent museum.

Museo Canario, Las Palmas ▷ **27** The whole history of Gran Canaria under one roof.

LAS PALMAS 20–44

Playa de las Canteras Museo Elder

Casa de Colón
Vegueta Catedral de Santa Ana
Museo Canario

ror Jardín Botánico Canario

Caldera de Bandama

THE NORTH 87–106

Barranco de Guayadeque

ortaleza Grande

THE SOUTH 45–70

a del Inglés

◄ ◄ ◄

9

Shopping

Gran Canaria provides a contrast of shopping experiences. On the one hand, there are modern shopping malls, duty-free outlets and designer stores, on the other artisan workshops, markets and small craft shops. Shopping centres dominate the south coast resorts, whereas Las Palmas offers major shopping streets with high street names and designer outlets, and some out-of-town malls. It is in the towns and larger villages where you will find authentic local products.

Canarian Classics

Ceramics are popular, and most of the products for sale on the island are made in the traditional manner, without a wheel, and to a traditional design. These are usually simple everyday objects such as plates, bowls and jugs. There are also some copies of pre-Hispanic artefacts such as the Idolo de Tara, the mother-earth fertility idol figurine. Centres of pottery making can be found at La Atalaya and Lugarejos. Baskets and basketware made from palm fronds and banana leaves are manufactured in Ingenio and Teror. Embroidered lace tablecloths are a specialty of the island and are made particularly at Ingenio, Agüimes and San Bartolomé de Tirajana. Bone-handled knives known as *naifes*, originally used by shepherds and workers in the banana plantations, are now collector's items and come with intricate carving and brass inlay. They are produced

TO MARKET, TO MARKET

Shopping in a Canarian market is one of the highlights of a trip to the island. Almost every town and large village has its weekly markets, some twice weekly, where local farmers sell their produce. In Las Palmas are the covered produce markets of Vegueta and the Mercado Central, and the flea market in San Telmo. In the south the fish market at Arguineguín is of particular note. For handicrafts and souvenirs try Santa Brígida, or Teror with its unusual religious artefacts, crafts and local foodstuffs.

From top: Ceramic pots at Teguise market; jewellery stall; packets of spices; straw hats and baskets

in Santa Maria de Guía and Gáldar and sold in the Fedac shops (▷ box). Other typically Canarian items include musical instruments such as the *timple* (a small four or five-string guitar) and *chácaras* (castanets), felt hats, and creams and soaps made from aloe vera, which grows extensively on the island.

Food and Drink to Bring Home

If you want to give a present that is typically Canarian, food options include the spicy sauce, *mojo*; cheese from Santa Maria de Guía, *queso de flor*; *bienmesabe* (almond syrup, also almond cake); *mazapan* (almond cake); banana and cactus jam; dried herbs; and almond biscuits from Tejeda. Drink options include the liqueurs *guindilla*, made from sour cherries in San Bartolomé and *mejunje*, made from rum, honey and lemons, from Santa Lucia; coffee beans from Agaete; Canarian wine and rum from Arucas.

Bargain Buys

The Canary Islands have retained their special status as a free trade zone, despite Spain's membership of the EU. There are minimal import duties and a low rate of VAT. Do bear in mind, however, that there are strict regulations governing how much can be exported for personal use (▷ 117). There are good bargains to be found for electronic goods, perfume, sunglasses, alcohol, tobacco and jewellery. Outlets selling these can be found in the main south coast resorts and in Las Palmas.

WHERE TO BUY SOUVENIRS

To buy your Canarian crafts you can either browse the many markets and small artisan shops throughout the island or go to one of the two Fedac shops. Fedac is the government sponsored, non-profit making organization that ensures your money goes direct to the craftsperson responsible for creating the item. There is a branch in Las Palmas (▷ 37) and one in the tourist information office in Playa del Inglés (▷ 65).

From top: Coffee beans; jewellery shop, Las Palmas; local goat's cheese; flower pots; rum from Arucas

Beaches

Many visitors are attracted to Gran Canaria by the blue skies, balmy temperatures and soft sands. The best beaches are generally in the south, but Las Canteras (▷ 29) in Las Palmas can match any of its counter-parts further down the coast, and there are also a few isolated gems to be discovered in unexpected parts of the island.

Jewels in the Crown

Gran Canaria has 236km (146 miles) of coast-line of which 60km (37 miles) are beaches. Some are long stretches of golden or dark sand running the length of a seafront promenade with excellent facilities, while others are small coves complete with a mountain backdrop. One thing they all have is common is clean, transparent blue waters. Few beaches can rival the golden dunes at Maspalomas (▷ 50–51)— but on the extreme southern tip the sea-swell can be strong. Playa del Inglés has an excellent beach backed by an attractive promenade and there is a section for nude bathing. The next beach travelling east is Las Burras, with calm waters that make it ideal for families. Further west Puerto Rico's gently curving beach is manmade with soft sand brought in from the Sahara. Again, it features safe bathing but it can get very crowded. The next cove along is Amadores, another fine artificial beach where ball games and radios are banned. Travelling west along the coast brings you to Puerto Mogán, with its delightful little bay of soft sand and shallow warm waters.

From top: Playa de las Canteras; Maspalomas dunes; Playa del Inglés; beach in peak season

PEACE AND QUIET

On the north coast, Sardina has a small beach beneath dark volcanic cliffs where the nearby rocks attract divers. Further round is the secluded cove of El Juncal, almost undiscovered by tourists, where the clear calm waters are enclosed by towering cliffs. The sheltered east coast cove at Aguas Dulces is ideal for snorkelling and diving and is often deserted; the one drawback is its proximity to the airport.

Gran Canaria by Night

Nightlife in Gran Canaria is concentrated in the larger resorts of the south and in Las Palmas, principally in hotels, where karaoke evenings and flamenco nights are common. Las Palmas has a thriving arts and music scene, and cinema is also popular. The island's casinos offer a more sophisticated way to spend the night, and there is always a local festival or carnival celebration somewhere on the island.

Clubs and Bars

In the southern resorts, discos and bars are generally in commercial centres such as the Yumbo Centre in Playa del Inglés, which has a lively gay and lesbian scene. Clubs don't get lively much before 11pm, and keep going until sunrise. There is something for everyone in Las Palmas—however mainstream or way out. Most of the trendiest clubs and bars are in the old town and around the marina. It is best to avoid the area around Santa Catalina late at night, known to have some less than desirable haunts. Remember, venues, clubs and discos change with every season so check ahead.

Romantic Evenings

If the raucous nightlife is not for you, the balmy evenings and beautiful settings provide many alternatives. For example, walking barefoot along the shoreline by the light of the stars, strolling on the promenade after a satisfying meal, or watching the sun go down over the mountains, are all the perfect end to a day.

From top: Clubbing; Kasbah shopping centre; Yumbo shopping centre; flamenco dancer; beach stroll

---

CASINOS

As well as the usual blackjack, roulette and slot machines, the casinos in Gran Canaria often stage a Las Vegas style dinner show. There are three casinos on the island: Casino Las Palmas (▷ 40) inside the Hotel Santa Catalina in Las Palmas; Casino Tamarindos (▷ 66) in the Hotel Meliá Tamarindos in San Agustín; and Gran Casino Costa Meloneras (✉ Avenida Mar Mediterráneo 1 ☎ 928 12 81 00; www.lopesanhotels.com).

Eating Out

Given the number of visitors here, it is no surprise that the island offers a wide range of eating options. Most restaurants have Canarian dishes on the menu, together with steaks, seafood dishes and Spanish favourites such as paella.

Where to Eat

Busy tourist resorts have a wide cross-section of restaurants, offering everything from English breakfast and hamburgers to pizzas and apple strudel. In the mountains, the most common type of restaurant is a *parrilla,* a country-style grill specializing in barbecued, grilled and roasted meat. In some areas restaurants have set up in the original Guanche caves, and these are a fascinating place to dine. Las Palmas boasts some upmarket restaurants, and tapas bars are very popular.

Local Specialties

Influenced by Spanish cooking, Canarian food has its own character based on local ingredients. Here are a few local delicacies:
• *conejo en salmorejo*—rabbit marinated in garlic and herbs, then basted in wine
• *gofio escaldado*—gofio (form of cereal) stirred into fish stock to produce a thick paste
• *papas arrugadas*—small potatoes boiled in their skins with salt, eaten with *mojo* sauce
• *puchero canario*—a hearty meat and vegetable casserole
• *ropa vieja*—chickpeas fried with diced meat and vegetables

PRACTICAL GUIDE

Many resort restaurants stay open all day to cater to demand but normal mealtimes may be adhered to in Las Palmas and remote areas. A good-value *menu del día*— three-course, fixed-price menu with drink—is often offered at lunch. Service has to be included in the price by law but if you are happy with the service an additional tip of 10 per cent is customary. There may also be a cover charge for items such as bread.

Eating out in Gran Canaria is a pleasure

Restaurants by Cuisine

While traditional Canarian cuisine is by far the most common on the island, resort areas and cities offer a wider variety. On this page restaurants are listed by cuisine. For a detailed description of each restaurant, see Gran Canaria by Area.

FINE DINING

Casa Montesdeoca (▷ 43)
El Cerdo Que Rie (▷ 43)
Faneque (▷ 106)
Los Guayres (▷ 69)
Qué Tal (▷ 70)

FISH/SEAFOOD

Apolo X1 (▷ 68)
Bar Cofradía de Pescadores (▷ 68)
Boccalino (▷ 68)
Cápita (▷ 105)
La Caracola: Seemuschel (▷ 68)
Casa Pepe (▷ 105)
Fragata (▷ 106)
La Marinera (▷ 44)
Miguelín (▷ 106)
Restaurante Cofradia (▷ 70)
Rias Bajas (▷ 70)
Terraza el Ancla (▷ 106)

FUSION/CONTEMPORARY

La Buena Vida (▷ 42)
Fusion Restaurant and Lounge Bar (▷ 69)
Mundo (▷ 70)

INTERNATIONAL

Anno Domini (▷ 68)
Candombe (▷ 42)
La Cantina (▷ 68)
Casa Carmelo (▷ 42)
Casa Romántica (▷ 105)
Los Cedros (▷ 43)
Galia (▷ 43)
El Novillo Precoz (▷ 44)
Restaurante Roma (▷ 44)

LIGHT MEALS

Café Santa Catalina (▷ 42)
Cañas y Tapas (▷ 42)
Chipi-Chipi (▷ 69)
El Faro (▷ 69)
Maximilian's (▷ 69)
Tea and Coffee Pot (▷ 44)
Tu Casa (▷ 70)

PIZZA/PASTA

Al Maccaroni (▷ 42)
Loopy's (▷ 44)
La Pasta Real (▷ 44)
La Pizza (▷ 44)

SPANISH

El Acueducto (▷ 42)
Café Madrid (▷ 42)
La Casa Vieja (▷ 68)
El Castillete (▷ 105)
La Cava Triana (▷ 43)
Las Cumbres Canarias (▷ 69)
La Foresta (▷ 69)

Gorbea (▷ 69)
Jardín Canario (▷ 106)
El Mesón de la Montana (▷ 106)
Mirador de Santa Lucia (▷ 86)
Patio Canario (▷ 70)
El Portalón (▷ 70)
La Veguetilla (▷ 106)

TRADITIONAL CANARIAN

Asadero Las Brasas (▷ 105)
Balcón de la Zamora (▷ 105)
Bodegón Vandama (▷ 105)
La Bodeguilla Juananá (▷ 68)
Casa Fataga (▷ 43)
La Cueva (▷ 105)
Cueva de la Tea (▷ 86)
La Esquina (▷ 86)
Las Grutas de Artiles (▷ 106)
La Hacienda del Molino (▷ 86)
Hao (▷ 86)
El Herreño (▷ 43)
Hoya la Vieja (▷ 43)
Restaurante La Albericoque (▷ 86)
Restaurant Centennial (▷ 86)
Tagoror (▷ 70)

If You Like...

However you'd like to spend your time in Gran Canaria, these ideas should help you tailor your perfect visit. Each suggestion has a fuller write-up elsewhere in the book.

SOMETHING FISHY

For innovative fish dishes and a personal service try La Caracola (▷ 68).
Enjoy sunset views and great seafood paella at La Marinera (▷ 43).
Dine in a traditional cave at La Cueva (▷ 105), one of Sardina's best fish restaurants.
Go to Arguineguín to eat fresh fish straight from the boat to your plate at Restaurante Cofradía (▷ 70).

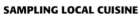

SAMPLING LOCAL CUISINE

Enjoy panoramic views while you dine at Balcón de la Zamora (▷ 105) near Teror.
Go back to traditional roots in Santa Lucia by eating Canarian cooking at La Hacienda del Molino (▷ 86).
Eat in interesting surroundings at La Silla in Artenara (▷ 75).
Fill up on local atmosphere as well as the food at the Hotel Madrid (▷ 109).

SAVING MONEY

Buy a *bono de guagua* bus pass (▷ 118) as soon as you arrive in Las Palmas.
Book a self-catering apartment (▷ 108), there are plenty to choose from in the south.
Take advantage of the reduced-tax shopping (▷ 38) on offer all over the island.
Take a picnic, the weather and landscape provide the perfect conditions.

STAYING BY THE BEACH

Relax in exquisite gardens at the Riu Grand Palace Maspalomas Oasis (▷ 112).
For beachfront decadence book the Hotel Reina Isabel (▷ 112) on Las Canteras beach.
Choose the intimate Hotel Puerto de Mogán (▷ 111), habourside at Puerto de Mogán.
The H10 Playa Meloneras Palace (▷ 112) combines modern elegance with traditional Canarian-style architecture.

From top: Paella; La Silla restaurant; picnic table; Puerto de Mogán

erto de Mogán

LIFE ON THE OCEAN WAVES

Sign up for windsurfing lessons at Club Mistral (▷ 66), Bahía Feliz.

See what's under the waves by learning to scuba dive with Dive Academy (▷ 66), Arguineguín.

Join Submarine Adventure (▷ 67) to get up close and personal with marine life.

Join the experts at Oceanside (▷ 40) for a spot of surfing.

surfing

FUN WITH THE KIDS

Take the family to Holiday World (▷ 59), where the fun continues on into the evening.

Play at being a cowboy—at Sioux City (▷ 61) there is plenty to keep the youngsters feeling lucky.

Cool the kids down at slip-sliding Aqualand (▷ 58).

Go to the beach (▷ 12); there are plenty of safe options to choose from.

BUYING LOCAL SOUVENIRS

Get an insight into the island's traditional crafts at the Playa del Inglés FEDAC store (▷ 64).

Buy an item of pottery made by local artists at La Atalaya (▷ 104).

Go to Arucas for your rum (▷ 104) and have a free taste before you buy.

Buy the genuine article at the Museum of Rocks (▷ 65) in Ingenio.

at the water park (above); rum (below)

GETTING IN TOUCH WITH THE PAST

Visit Museo Canario (▷ 27) for an insight into the prehistory of Gran Canaria.

Explore cave dwellings and traces of ancient civilizations along the Barranco de Guayadeque (▷ 48–49).

Go back to colonial times with a stroll through the showpiece town of Teror (▷ 96–97).

See how early Guanches lived at the Mundo Aborigen (▷ 53) open-air museum.

A MORE ACTIVE LIFE

Hire a bike and cycle the Caldera de Bandama (▷ 90–91).
Go hiking in the Tamadaba (▷ 81) pine forest, a paradise for keen hikers.
Imagine you have been transported to the Sahara Desert on the back of a camel (▷ 66).
Play a round of golf (▷ 66) at one of the island's superb courses.

A GOOD NIGHT OUT

Have a drink by the harbour in Puerto de Mogán (▷ 56–57) and watch the sun set behind the cliffs.
Try your luck at the wheel in the Casino de Las Palmas (▷ 40).
Hit the dance floor at Pacha (▷ 40), the hottest club in town.
Combine dinner with a show at Garbo's Dinner Show (▷ 67).

Barranco de Guayadeque

GETTING BACK TO NATURE

View plant species endemic to the island all in one place at Jardín Botánico (▷ 94–95).
Discover the huge number of cactuses thriving on Gran Canaria at Cactualdea (▷ 61).
Smell the pine as you stroll through the Pinar de Tamadaba (▷ 81).
Bare all at the Dunas de Maspalomas (▷ 50) nature reserve.

Golf at Maspalomas

BEING PAMPERED

Treat yourself to a treatment at the spa in the Gloria Palace San Agustín (▷ 110).
Indulge in 5-star luxury at the Lopesan Villa del Conde (▷ 112).
Eat at the most elegant restaurant in Las Palmas, Casa Montesdeoca (▷ 43), where formal waiters tend your every need.
Stay at a luxury rural retreat such as La Hacienda del Buen Suceso (▷ 112).

Out on the town (above); Jardín Botánico (below)

Gran Canaria by Area

LAS PALMAS

THE SOUTH

CENTRAL GRAN CANARIA

THE NORTH

Las Palmas

The capital of Gran Canaria often gets overlooked but it is well worth a visit. Stroll the streets of the old quarter with its typical Canarian buildings, check out the designer shops of Triana and the Avenida Mesa y López, or treat yourself to a day on the golden sands of Las Canteras beach.

LAS PALMAS

249 ▲
Montaña del Faro

La Isleta

Punta del Confital

Playa del Confital

Castillo de la Luz

Playa de las Canteras

Museo Elder

Parque de Santa Catalina

Bahía del Confital

Playa de las Alcaravaneras

GC2

GC1

Ciudad Jardín

GC23

Museo Néstor

Parque Doramas

Pueblo Canario

■ Las Torres Altas

Parque San Telmo

GC300

Casa de Colón

Casa Museo de Pérez Galdós

Cátedral de Santa Ana

GC3

Vegueta

GC23

Museo Canario

Lomo Blanco ■

GC3

GC110

GC31

Pedro Hidalgo ■

GC115

Playa la Lay

GC3

0 _____ 2 km
0 _____ 1 mile

I

2

3

4

J

K

Playa del Cebadel

Caletón

rcado de Vegueta
ntro Atlántico
Arte Moderno (CAAM)

L   M

Casa de Colón

HIGHLIGHTS

● Reconstruction of the poop deck of the *Nina*
● Reconstruction of Columbus's cabin in board the *Santa Maria*
● Copies of Columbus's early charts and instruments
● Columbus's logbook
● Model ships
● Nautical maps
● Early Las Palmas history
● Paintings from the Prado
● The crypt

This is one of the oldest houses in Las Palmas and probably where Columbus stayed when he visited the city in the late 15th century. To tread in the footsteps of the great explorer is quite a thrill.

Traditional architecture Casa de Colón is a fine example of early Canarian building and was one of the first houses to be completed following the Spanish Conquest of 1478. Built around two elegant stone courtyards, and with its attractive wooden balconies, carved stone portals and ornamentation, it made a fine governor's residence and is worth a visit for the building alone.

Charting the world The building now houses a museum dedicated to early exploration, Columbus and the history of Las Palmas. Gran Canaria

Bust of Christopher Columbus outside the Casa de Colón (left); the carved balconies and ornamental doorway are typical of early Canarian architecture (middle); portrait of Columbus (right)

proved to be a strategic island and a natural base for refuelling when the early explorers undertook their voyages to find the New World. Columbus stopped here on his way to discover Cuba during his first voyage of 1492. On the ground floor you can learn about his exploits, see the nautical charts and instruments, and view model ships and recon-structions of parts of Columbus's ships.

History and art Upstairs don't miss the model of 17th-century Las Palmas, complemented by historical material about the city. There is also a collection of 16th- to 20th-century paintings on loan from the Prado Museum in Madrid. Be sure not to miss the crypt, which is devoted to the pre-Columbian period, including some fine Ecuadorean and Mexican pottery, plus basketware from the 20th-century Yanomani Indians of Brazil.

THE BASICS

www.casadecolon.com
➕ c5
✉ Calle Colón 1
☎ 928 31 23 73
🕐 Mon–Fri 9–7, Sat–Sun 9–3
🚌 1, 2, 3, 9, 12, 13
♿ Good on ground floor
✋ Free

Catedral de Santa Ana

TOP 25

Plaza Santa Ana (left); chapter house mosaic floor (middle); bell tower (right)

HIGHLIGHTS

● The façade
● The Patio de los Naranjos
● *Stations of the Cross* by Jésus Arencibia, in the Diocesan Museum
● Grand tombs

TIP

● Take the lift up to the viewing platform then climb the bell tower for some of the best views over the old town, in particular the Plaza de Santa Ana.

Work started on the only ecclesiastical masterpiece in the Canaries in 1497, and took some 400 years to complete. The result is a mishmash of styles—Gothic, Renaissance, baroque and neoclassical —with a dash of local Canarian influence.

Soaring space The interior of the building is a delight, and a light and airy relief after the rather sombre, if imposing, façade. Entering through a 16th-century doorway you experience a sense of grandeur and space. The three lofty naves are full of light and the grey basalt columns and wooden vaulting complete the picture.

Tombs, paintings and sculptures The side chapels contain the tombs of various bishops as well as the poet Bartolomé Cairasco (1538– 1610), the historian José de Viera y Clavijo (1731–1813) and the diplomat Fernando de León y Castillo (1842–1918), whose names you will see replicated in street signs and squares in the city. Baroque paintings flank the altar and beneath the dome are figures of saints sculpted by Luján Pérez, the artist responsible for remodelling the cathedral façade in the late 19th century.

Museo Diocesano de Arte Sacro A visit to the Diocesan Museum, accessed through a charming courtyard, the Patio de los Naranjos, is included in the entrance fee. Items of religious art are on display, including valuable sculptures and paintings from the 15th and 16th centuries, as well as gold and silverware.

Museo Canario

This is an excellent museum with a serious message concerning the prehistory of the island, its early people and their environment. Follow the story from neolithic times through to European conquest and colonisation in the 15th century.

Guanche society The first inhabitants of the Canary Islands were the Guanche people of North African Berber origin, who lived in Gran Canaria between 500BC and AD1500. These people were cave dwellers, although they did go on to build stone houses. They kept livestock, grew and ground barley, harvested shellfish and made jewellery using conch shells. They also mummified their dead, indicating a link between the Gaunches and the ancient Egyptians.

The effects of conquest Imagine the shock of the arrival of the Spanish to the Guanches' homeland. They had never seen a horse and had no knowledge of metal. At first they were trusting of their new visitors but once the Spaniards realized they lacked proper weapons they set about invading and enslaving them. The Guanches put up a good fight but were finally defeated in 1483.

In the museum The museum was founded in 1879 by Dr Gregorio Chil and consists of 11 galleries spread over two floors. The final galleries contain pre-Hispanic pottery that can be linked to pottery-making on the island today. The Guanches had no potter's wheel; instead they used bones, shells and bamboo sticks to shape the clay.

THE BASICS

www.elmuseocanario.com
🔲 c5
✉ Calle Dr. Verneau 2
☎ 928 33 68 00
🕐 Mon–Fri 10–8, Sat–Sun 10–2
🚌 1, 2, 3, 9, 12, 13
♿ Good
💶 Inexpensive
❓ Guided tours available—check for times

HIGHLIGHTS

● Guanche dwellings
● Mummies
● Idol of Tara, the earth goddess
● Ceramics
● Collection of old maps
● Macabre skulls
● Shop selling Guanche-related artefacts

TIP

● Purchase a guidebook at the beginning of your visit as the labels on the displays are in Spanish only while the book has English translations.

Museo Elder

The exhibits invite experimentation (left); exterior of the museum (right)

THE BASICS

www.museoelder.org
➕ b1
✉ Parque de Santa Catalina
☎ 828 01 18 28
🕐 Tue–Sun 10–8 (Jul-Aug 11–9)
🍴 Café in museum
🚌 1, 2, 3, 12, 30, 32, 42, 43
♿ Good
👆 Moderate
❓ Good range of temporary exhibits

HIGHLIGHTS

● *Ariane V* space rocket
● F5 fighter plane
● Classic cars and locomotive
● Bubble Planetarium
● Cinemax'70
● Chicks hatching

This is the museum where it is positively forbidden not to touch. Here is your chance to explore science and technology first hand as you are the central character in the exhibition.

Fun for all the family If you have the misfortune to get rain on your visit to Las Palmas, this is an excellent alternative to the beach. You may think 'hands-on' museums are geared mainly towards children but the Museo Elder really does have something for everyone.

What to see The museum has over 200 exhibits (all labelled in English as well as Spanish), nearly all of which encourage the visitor to interact by pushing buttons, pulling levers and playing games. On the ground floor there are planes, trains and boats. Step inside the cockpit of an Airbus or a F5 fighter and operate its controls. View the *Ariane V* space rocket and learn about satellites, weather and types of energy. There is also a section on classic cars and steam locomotives. On the next floor check out the Bubble Planetarium and see the stars. Learn about mechanics, optics, sound, waves, electricity and magnetism. Take a look at the biology and medicine section complete with a greenhouse. You can also see how chicks are born and, if you are lucky, actually see one hatch out.

Other options The large screen Cinemax'70 on the top floor is unique in the Canary Islands and screens films in English. There are also regular temporary exhibitions.

Sun umbrellas for hire (left); apartment blocks and hotels line the beach (right)

TOP 25

Playa de las Canteras

Few cities can boast such a large expanse of fine, golden sand within minutes of the main shopping streets. Playa de las Canteras was drawing visitors long before the south coast resorts took off.

City beach Playa de las Canteras, at 3km (2 miles) long, marks the northwestern edge of Las Palmas. Its waters are kept warm and sheltered by the natural rock barrier, La Barra, which breaks the incoming waves, turning the sea into a warm, shallow lagoon at low tide. Where the reef runs out at the southwest end of the beach and the sand becomes black, the sea is more challenging and this is where the surfers hang out.

Along the promenade Whether you enjoy walking, jogging, rollerblading, people-watching or just chilling out at a restaurant, bar or café, the promenade at Las Canteras is a place everyone can enjoy. The wide walkway is totally free of traffic and the perfect spot to stroll or have lunch after a morning at the shops. The evening is a pleasant time for a pre-dinner amble and there is a tempting array of excellent restaurants to try.

Staying near the beach Although the weather tends to be more cloudy in the north of Gran Canaria, it doesn't stop a large number of visitors and locals from spending time at this beach. There are numerous hotels and apartments, many with good sea views, within a stone's throw of the promenade, and staying in Las Palmas is an interesting alternative to a holiday in the south.

THE BASICS

➕ a1
✉ Playa de las Canteras
🍴 Cafés and restaurants line the promenade
🚌 1, 2, 3, 12, 13, 20, 41
🚢 Boats to Cádiz on Spanish mainland, jetfoil to Tenerife and ferries to all Canarian islands from passenger port

HIGHLIGHTS

● Clean, large expanse of sandy beach
● Safe swimming
● Promenade
● Surfing and body boarding at southwest end
● Bars and restaurants

LAS PALMAS

★ TOP 25

Vegueta

HIGHLIGHTS

- Mercado de Vegueta
- Catedral de Santa Ana
- Streets around the cathedral
- Shops selling Canarian products
- Casa de Colón
- Museo Canario

TIP

- Start your visit early at the Mercado de Vegueta, which opens at 6.30am Monday to Saturday.

Take a stroll among the picturesque streets of Las Palmas' old town, centred round the imposing Catedral de Santa Ana. Here you will find the greatest concentration of historic buildings in the city.

To market This is the most pleasant district of Las Palmas to stroll around. Starting with a visit to the covered market (▷ 33), the oldest in the city, you will be amazed by the variety of produce—fish, meat, fruit and vegetables all neatly displayed. It's a good place to try *churros*, a fried dough stick or coil dipped in sugar and traditionally eaten by the Spanish as a treat for breakfast.

Peaceful quarter Away from the bustle of the market the most prominent building in Vegueta is the cathedral (▷ 26). The attractive square

Clockwise from far left: Plaza Cairasco; old houses line the streets; façade in Plaza de Santa Ana; red-washed walls; bust in front of the Gabinete Literario in Plaza Cairasco; Patio de los Naranjos in the Catedral de Santa Ana

opposite, the palm-lined Plaza de Santa Ana, guarded by two groups of bronze dogs, provides a quiet resting place and a fine view of the cathedral's façade. Behind the cathedral is the Casa de Colón (▷ 24–25), visited by Christopher Columbus before his explorations in the late 15th century. Wandering around the nearby streets you will find delightful smaller squares and quiet cobbled streets lined with post-conquest buildings. Flowers trail from wooden balconies in streets such as Calle de los Balcones, Calle Herrería and Calle Mendizábal. While in this district, you can visit the Museo Canario (▷ 27) for a glimpse of early Canarian life dating back to neolithic and Guanche times. There are also some good restaurants in the area and shops selling authentic Canarian products. Calle Pelota is fast becoming the 'in' place for trendy bars.

THE BASICS

✚ c5

✉ Old town; the streets immediately south of the GC110 Carretera Pico Viento

🍴 Many cafés, bars and restaurants in the area

🚌 1, 2, 3, 9, 12, 13

More to See

CASA MUSEO DE PÉREZ GALDÓS

www.casamuseoperezgaldos.com
This typically Canarian 18th-century house was the birthplace of the 'Spanish Dickens', Bentio Pérez Galdós, the Canary Islands' greatest and most famous novelist. The house contains an extensive collection of documents, books, furniture and personal effects belonging to the writer.
➕ c5 ✉ Calle Cano 2–6 ☎ 928 36 69 76 🕐 Tue–Fri 10–2, 4–8, Sat–Sun 10–2 🚌 1, 2, 3 ♿ Few 💷 Free ❓ Guided tours only on the hour

CASTILLO DE LA LUZ

The Castillo de la Luz (Castle of Light) is in a small park in the south of La Isleta at the top end of the city. It was built in 1541 to defend the city's natural harbour but was burned out during the invasion of Dutch pirates in 1599. It was subsequently rebuilt, extended and improved and in 1941 declared a national historic monument. Restored in 1990, the Castillo today serves as a cultural centre.

➕ K2 ✉ Calle Juan Rejón s/n ☎ 928 44 68 24 (tourist information) 🕐 Check with tourist information 🍽 Café in the park 🚌 1, 2, 3 ♿ Call for details

CENTRO ATLÁNTICO DE ARTE MODERNO (CAAM)

www.caam.net
The Centro Atlántico de Arte Moderno (CAAM) is Las Palmas' principal art gallery. The permanent collection displays the work of contemporary Spanish and some Canarian artists. Around the corner in Plaza de San Antonio Abad CAAM has another gallery exhibiting the work of young Canarian artists.
➕ c5 ✉ Calle de los Balcones 9–11 ☎ 928 31 18 00 🕐 Tue–Sat 10–9, Sun 10–2 🍽 Café 🚌 1, 2, 3, 9, 12, 13 ♿ Good 💷 Free

CIUDAD JARDÍN

'Garden City' is Las Palmas' leafy suburb, and was created by British merchants in the 19th century. At its heart is the Parque Doramas, home to the Pueblo Canario (▷ 34)

CAAM's clean white lines are a perfect setting for modern art

Paintings by Jose Rosales in the Castillo de la Luz

and the grand Hotel Santa Catalina (▷ 112) with its fine restaurant and smart casino (▷ 40).

➕ a3 ✉ Parque Doramas and surrounding streets 🚌 1, 2, 3 ♿ Good

LA ISLETA

This barren, volcanic peninsula at the northern end of the city is rather desolate but has some good surfing beaches and great views. The Isleta has traditionally been a popular neighbourhood for fishermen and working people, mainly employees of the nearby Puerto de la Luz.

➕ K1 ✉ Northern end of Las Palmas 🚌 41 from Parque Santa Catalina

MERCADO DE VEGUETA

Produce markets bring colour to any city and Las Palmas' oldest market is no exception. The 1854 building is packed with attractively presented fruit, vegetables, fish and meat. The variety of potatoes alone is amazing.

➕ c5 ✉ Calle Mendizábal 1 🕐 Mon–Thu 6.30–2, Fri–Sat 6.30–3 🍴 Cafés close by 🚌 1, 2, 3, 50, 51, 52 ♿ Good 🖐 Free

MUSEO NÉSTOR

www.museonestor.com

Part of the Pueblo Canario (▷ 34), the Museo Néstor displays the works of the island's most famous painter, Néstor Martín Fernández de la Torre (1887–1938). He had a passionate love for the environment and a strong desire to protect the natural elements of Gran Canaria. His best-known work is *El Poema del Atlántico,* a celebration of the island's ocean environment.

➕ b3 ✉ Ciudad Jardín ☎ 928 24 51 35 🕐 Tue–Sat 10–8, Sun 10.30–2.30 🍴 Café in Pueblo Canario 🚌 1 ♿ None 🖐 Inexpensive

PARQUE DORAMAS

Named after the last Guanche king of eastern Gran Canaria, this park contains the Museo Néstor (▷ above), Pueblo Canario (▷ 34) and Hotel Santa Catalina (▷ 112). It is a pleasant, shady place to while away an afternoon away from the city crowds.

➕ b3 ✉ Ciudad Jardín 🍴 Café in Pueblo Canario 🚌 1, 12, 13

House decorations at Pueblo Canario

Néstor's El Mediodía (Midday), *1921–3, part of his* Poema del Atlántico *series*

PARQUE DE SANTA CATALINA

Santa Catalina is really more of a city square than a park and is a hive of activity, both day and night. The local men play chess and dominoes beneath the palm trees, while tourists mingle with traders, seamen and shoeshine boys. The excellent Museo Elder (▷ 28) stands in the square, and there's also a tourist information kiosk. This is the red-light district, so be wary at night.

🚹 b1 ✉ Santa Catalina 🍴 Several cafés in the park 🚌 1, 2, 3, 12, 13, 41

PARQUE SAN TELMO

Perfectly placed for a spot of relaxation among its shady palms after hitting the shops in Triana, the park's delightful *modernista* café is popular with locals and visitors alike. The pretty church, the Ermita de San Telmo, is another feature. The bus terminus and taxi rank make this an important transport centre.

🚹 c4 ✉ Corner of Calle Bravo Murillo and Avenida Rafael Cabrera 🍴 Kiosk café 🚌 1, 11, 41

PLAYA DE LAS ALCARAVANERAS

This beach may not be quite in the same league as Las Canteras and is somewhat marred by its proximity to the port and the marina, but it is still popular with locals and has a good stretch of golden sand. The cleanliness of the water is dubious—you might prefer to stick to sunbathing.

🚹 b2 ✉ Alcaravaneras 🍴 Snack bars on beach 🚌 12, 13

PUEBLO CANARIO

When designing this 'village' the intention of modernist artist Néstor Martín Fernández de la Torre was not to attract tourists but to preserve Canarian culture. The strong tradition of Canarian music and dance, together with authentic costume, is kept alive with regular shows every week (▷ 41). There's a restaurant and shops selling Canarian crafts.

🚹 b3 ✉ Parque Doramas ☎ 928 24 35 93 ⏰ Tue–Sat 10–8, Sun 10.30–2.30 👆 Free 🍴 Restaurant 🚌 1, 12, 13 ♿ Good ❓ Performances Sun 11.30

Playing chess in Parque de Santa Catalina

Modernista café in Parque San Telmo

Historic Las Palmas

Stroll past the designer shops of Triana, soak up the atmosphere of the old quarter and return to the square made famous by Franco.

DISTANCE: 2km (1.2 miles)   **ALLOW:** 1.5 hours strolling, 4 hours with stops

START

PARQUE DE SAN TELMO
➕ c4 🚌 1, 2, 3

END

PLAZA DE CAIRASCO
➕ c5 🚌 2, 3, 30, 90

❶ Start with a coffee in the lovely *modernista* kiosk café in Parque San Telmo, then walk south on pedestrianized Calle Mayor de Triana. Note the art nouveau buildings, starting at No. 98.

❽ Rest here in the delightful Hotel Madrid (No. 2), where Franco spent the night and declared the onset of the Spanish Civil War from the balcony of room 3 in 1936.

❷ Check out the shops along the way and at the end angle left at the statue of Juan Negrín. At the major highway, go one block left to Teatro Pérez Galdós (▷ 41). Retrace your steps and cross over to the market (▷ 33) on the left.

❼ Passing the museum, continue 60m (66yd) up Calle Dr Chil then angle sharply back into Plaza Santa Ana opposite the cathedral. Carry on down the hill and cross the highway and on into Plaza de Cairasco.

❸ Carry on up Calle Mendizábal, turn right up Calle de los Balcones. Here on the left you can visit CAAM modern art gallery (▷ 32).

❻ Retrace your steps to the end of Espiritu Santo. Turn left into Calle Reloj and walk to Calle Dr Chil. Turn right. The Museo Canario (▷ 27) is on the left.

❹ At the end turn right and follow through to the left to Calle Colón and the Casa de Colón (▷ 24–25). Continue to the end of Calle Colón and turn left passing the cathedral façade.

❺ The cathedral museum (▷ 26) is 25m (27yd) left at the next turning, in Espiritu Santo.

Shopping

ATARECOS
Bright clothing from around the world is on offer at this small boutique, along with zany jewellery and craftwork. This is not a typical Canarian clothing store but you can pick some unusual and individual ethnic choices and some local handicraft items.
➕ c5 ✉ Calle Cano 30
🚌 1, 2, 3

BENETTON
There are three branches of this popular Italian chain in Las Palmas—one in Triana (the old town), and the other two on the main shopping street, Avenida Mesa y Lopez, not too far from the beach. All the usual colourful items are displayed beautifully for both adults and children.
➕ c4 ✉ Calle Mayor de Triana 77 ☎ 928 37 40 12
🚌 8, 80, 82, 83, 91

BOUTIQUE GEMA
Come here for classic one-off designs aimed at 30-somethings. The clothes are modern, smart and what well-dressed Las Palmas women like to be seen in.
➕ c5 ✉ Calle Travieso 13
☎ 928 36 27 79 🚌 1, 2, 3

BOUTIQUE IBIO
Stylish Italian fashion for a younger clientele. Animal prints from Roberto Cavalli, brightly coloured handbags and trendy accessories including the latest in sunglasses. Casual clothing includes T-shirts and up-to-the-minute trainers.
➕ c4 ✉ Calle Viera y Clavijo 6 ☎ 928 36 09 80 🚌 2, 3, 8, 82, 83, 84

BOXES & CIGARS
Everything for the cigar aficionado—the quality is guaranteed and the choice is huge. If it is for a present, the box is as good as the cigar within.
➕ a1 ✉ Calle Ripoche 10
☎ 928 26 71 78 🚌 1, 2, 3, 45, 47

CASA RICARDO
At the south end of the main shopping street in Triana, this is where you can buy confectionery to

OUT OF TOWN
Malls are popular in Las Palmas, a mix of shopping and entertainment. The newest, El Muelle in the port area, is housed in an abstract glass building on the water's edge. Two floors include Spanish chain stores such as Cortifel alongside well-known international names such as The Body Shop, C & A and Timberland. Las Arenas mall is located at the west end of Las Canteras beach with shops covering fashion, traditional gifts, books and more. The biggest mall, with over 100 shops and a hypermarket, is La Bellena, 3km (2 miles) out of town on the road to Teror.

take home. A shop dedicated to the pick-and-mix type of candies—bonbons, lollipops and liquorice.
➕ c5 ✉ Corner Calle Mayor de Triana and Calle Losero
☎ 928 36 73 73 🚌 8, 80, 82, 83, 91

EL CORTE INGLÉS
www.elcorteingles.es
Spain's premier department store is located in the main shopping street in Las Palmas and occupies both sides of the street. You can buy just about anything you should need, from local produce to furniture, electrical goods to clothes and books. Fashion for all the family is located on the north side of the street, household and electronics on the south side. The top-floor café in the north branch serves a decent coffee and a light lunch when you've had enough of shopping.
➕ a2 ✉ Avenida Mesa y López 18 ☎ 928 26 30 00
🚌 3, 44, 45, 46, 47, 30

CUMBRES CANARÍAS
A deli offering tasty ingredients to fill your sandwiches. Smoked hams hang from the ceiling, local sausages, bread, olives and cheeses from around the island are piled high on the counter; this shop is thronged with locals, a good enough reason to buy.
➕ a1 ✉ Calle Tomás Miller 47–49 ☎ 928 47 22 46
🚌 1, 2, 3, 45, 47

FEDAC

www.fedac.org
This attractively displayed shop is the outlet for the government-sponsored, non-profit-making organization that sees your money is paid directly to the individual artisan. Products include pottery, lace, knives, jewellery, basketware and musical instruments. You can even buy a mini version of the traditional Canarian wooden balcony.

➕ c4 ✉ Calle Domingo J Navarro 7 ☎ 928 36 96 61 🚌 8, 80, 82, 83, 84, 91

EL GABINETE GASTRONÓMICO

A traditional bodega where you can buy Spanish and Canarian wine, rum and tobacco products. They also import spirits from outside Spain.

➕ c5 ✉ Calle Torres 18 ☎ 928 38 04 43 🚌 8, 54, 82, 83, 84, 91

IDIOMÁTIKA

www.idiomatika.net
This bookshop specializes in foreign-language books and has a good range of English titles. You can browse through the reference books and check out the lastest novels to read on the beach. Also stocks language CDs and dictionaries.

➕ b4 ✉ Calle Senador Castillo Olivares 52 ☎ 928 43 32 65 🚌 2, 3, 80, 82, 83, 84, 90, 91

LA LIBRERÍA

www.libreriedelcabildo.com
A serious government-run bookshop with plenty of information on Gran Canaria—from music to hiking—mostly in Spanish but you can find a few translations if you search. Also has walking maps and CDs of Canarian music.

➕ c5 ✉ Calle Cano 24 ☎ 928 38 15 39 🚌 8, 54, 82, 83, 84, 91

MARKS & SPENCER

Home-from-home shopping at this well-known British department store, if you want to buy any of your favourite items.

➕ a2 ✉ Avenida Mesa y López 32 ☎ 928 22 69 63 🚌 3, 44, 45, 46, 47, 30

MERCADO CENTRAL

Striking with its faded red façade complete with

FREE TRADE POLICY

As a free-trade island, you can certainly pick up bargains in Las Palmas. For perfume and cosmetics check out the chain stores Maya, Defa and Yves Rocher; all have branches throughout the city. If it is electronic goods you are after, the Visanta chain offer competitive prices (www.visanta-es. com). And for tobacco try Juan Marquez (Calle Ripoche 1) for a range of cigarettes, cigars of all sizes and packs of loose tobacco.

---

flags, inside the attractive market stalls are set up on a black and beige checked tiled floor. This is considered the next best food market after Mercado de Vegueta, and it is well placed close to the main shopping street of Avenida Mesa y López.

➕ a2 ✉ Calle Galicia 40 🕐 Closed Sun 🚌 3, 44, 45, 46, 47, 30

MERCADO DE VEGUETA

See page 33.

MIGUEL CRESPO

Housed in a charming old building in a lovely square close to the cathedral, this shop is devoted to the aloe vera plant. Aloe vera is grown throughout Gran Canaria and is the base ingredient for a plethora of soaps, creams and potions used for both healing and beauty. Second branch at Calle General Vives 4.

➕ c5 ✉ Plaza San Antonio Abad 5 ☎ 928 32 08 56 🚌 1, 2, 3, 9, 12, 13

MORALES

This traditional *pasteleria* and café tempts the taste buds with an array of delicious cakes and pastries. The window displays are works of art and often feature festivals or events such as Easter, weddings or Christmas. Good selection of sweets, too.

➕ c4 ✉ Calle Viera y Clavijo 4 ☎ 928 38 41 60 🚌 2, 3, 8, 82, 83, 84

NARA

www.naraonline.com

A family-run business stocking popular lines of china and porcelain figurines, glass objects d'art and watches, including well-known names such as Lladro, Swarovski and Lalique. There are also branches in Maspalomas and San Agustín.

➕ a1 ✉ Calle Tomás Miller ☎ 928 26 09 28 🚌 1, 2, 3, 45, 47

NATURA SELECTION

One of a chain of shops selling Fairtrade clothing made of silk and cotton from around the globe. They also stock lots of gift ideas such as candles, crafts and jewellery.

➕ c4 ✉ Calle Mayor de Triana 92 ☎ 928 36 75 06 🚌 8, 80, 82, 83, 91

ORBIS

If you want to buy a *timple,* a type of Canarian guitar (▷ panel), there are plenty to choose from here. You can have one custom made, but it will not be cheap. Other musical instruments and Canarian music CDs are also available.

➕ c5 ✉ Calle Mayor de Triana 51 ☎ 928 36 81 48 🚌 8, 80, 82, 83, 91

LAS PALMITAS

Enter this charming little shop through the tiny doorway close to the cathedral. It's an excellent place for buying Canarian crafts. The shop is packed to the gunnels with every type of Canarian traditional costume, local foodstuffs, including spicy *mojo* sauce and local jams, plus ceramics and bone-handled knives.

➕ c5 ✉ Calle Herreria 7 ☎ 928 33 26 33 🚌 1, 2, 3, 9, 12, 13

PUEBLO CANARIO

When you have had a stroll around Doramas Park and visited the Museo Néstor (▷ 33), take the chance, while you're in the area, to buy some authentic Canarian souvenirs or crafts from the shops in the lovingly created Canarian village (▷ 34). Choose from decorative folk costumes, T-shirts, pottery, books and CDs of Canarian music.

➕ b3 ✉ Parque Doramas ☎ 928 24 35 93 🚌 1, 12, 13

CANARIAN MUSIC

Traditional Canarian music and dance has seen something of a revival since the 1970s, particularly through the music of the island's most popular group, Los Gofiones. Musical items for sale include the *timple,* a small four- or five-string guitar and the *chacara,* the Canarian castenet, as well as CDs of traditional folk music. See Orbis (▷ left) for all your musical needs.

EL PUENTE

With a window full of every type of Canarian traditional costume, this is the place to come for the complete outfit, plus hats—both straw and felt—and other accessories. Also tablecloths, other embroidered items and pottery.

➕ c5 ✉ Calle General Bravo 26 🚌 2, 3, 80, 82, 83, 84, 90, 91

EL TALLER

The pick 'n' mix of the jewellery world, this company has shops throughout the Canary Islands and in mainland Spain. You can buy every colour and every design of bead or stone to make your own jewellery and all colours of leather on which to string them. The vivid window display perfectly illustrates the wide selection.

➕ a2 ✉ Calle Leo Tolstoy 26 ☎ 928 26 21 27 🚌 3, 44, 45, 46, 47, 30

ZARA

www.zara.com

There are several branches of this popular Spanish clothes store aimed at the fashion-conscious young woman. At this branch there is plenty of choice in all the latest styles at a reasonable price.

➕ c5 ✉ Calle Mayor de Triana 31 ☎ 928 36 80 88 🚌 8, 80, 82, 83, 91

Entertainment and Activities

ENTERTAINMENT AND ACTIVITIES

LAS PALMAS

AUDITORIO ALFREDO KRAUS

www.auditorio-alfredokraus.com

Located at the west end of Las Canteras beach, not only do you get some excellent cultural events and concerts, you get wonderful sea views as well. Named after the distinguished tenor Alfredo Kraus, who was born in the city in 1927, it was opened in 1997.

➕ Off map at a2 ✉ Paseo de las Canteras s/n ☎ 928 49 17 70 ⏰ Ticket office Mon–Fri 10–2, 4.30–8.30, Sat 10–2 🚌 25, 35, 31

CASINO DE LAS PALMAS

www.casinolaspalmas.com

Casino in the Hotel Santa Catalina where you can play baccarat, blackjack and roulette amid smart surroundings. Dress is formal—men are expected to wear a tie—and you will need to take your passport for ID.

➕ b3 ✉ Hotel Santa Catalina, León y Castillo 227 ☎ 928 23 39 08 ⏰ Sun–Thu 4pm–4am, Fri–Sat 4pm–5am 🚌 1, 17

CLIQUOT

Down in the old town, this bar is the place to come and listen to Spanish-Latino pop music. There's a balcony where you can watch the dancers down below. Gets very lively and crowded with a slightly older clientele.

➕ c5 ✉ Calle Mesa de León 3 ☎ 928 49 25 85 ⏰ Mon–Sat 11pm–4am 🚌 1, 13

DISCOTECA DOJO

Dojo pumps out R & B, top 40 hits, house, rock and more. Watch out for special themed nights and party nights.

➕ a1 ✉ Calle Presidente Alvear 69 ☎ 928 49 29 85 ⏰ Thu–Sat until late 🚌 1, 12, 45, 46, 47

CUASQUÍAS

www.cuasquias.com

Live performances of modern music including jazz, Latin, funk, rock and soul. It does get crowded at the weekends. The bar opens around 7pm every day except Sunday and there is a menu of traditional Canarian cuisine; tapas are also available.

SERIOUS ENTERTAINMENT

Some prestigious festivals take place in Las Palmas throughout the year. In January and early February the International Music Festival is held with concerts staged at the Auditorio Alfredo Kraus. Opera is celebrated with a dedicated festival in March and April and features special performances of the Spanish light operettas known as *zarzuelas*. In July the International Festival of Ballet and Dance presents a varied programme.

There are a pool tables in the glazed courtyard.

➕ c5 ✉ Calle San Pedro 2 ☎ 928 38 38 40 ⏰ Tue–Sat 11pm–3am, live music starts around 12.30am 🚌 1, 2, 3, 13

GALERIA DE ARTE MONOPOL

This small centre opposite the university library has a few outside terrace bars and restaurants. Inside the shopping is limited but there is a cinema, bars and a couple of clubs. Definitely a student domain—things don't liven up until after midnight and keep on rocking until the early hours.

➕ c5 ✉ Plaza de Hurtado de Mendoza/Calle San Pedro ☎ 655 55 49 79 🚌 1, 2, 3, 13

OCEANSIDE

www.ocean-side.es

Book a surfing lesson or a course of lessons. There's a comprehensive surf shop and lots of surfing-related videos and events.

➕ Off map at a2 ✉ Calle Almansa 14 ☎ 928 22 04 37 🚌 35, 47

PACHA

www.pacha.com

This world-famous chain opened here in 1987 and keeps on rocking as popular as ever, especially with the not quite so youthful crowd. Wide range of music, plus fashion shows and beauty contests.

➕ a2 ✉ Calle Simón
Bolivar 3 ☎ 928 27 16 84
🕐 Tue–Sun times vary, check
for details 🚌 1, 12, 13, 41

LAS PALMERAS GOLF CLUB

www.laspalmerasgolf.com
A fantastic new 18-hole
course and sports resort
just behind the western
end of Las Canteras
beach and near the Las
Arenas Shopping Centre.
With great views of the
beach and the sea, you
can play all 18 holes,
or settle for 9, have a
go on the driving range
or take a lesson. The
spa complex opened in
December 2008.
➕ Off map at a2 ✉ Avenida
Dr Alfonso Chiscano Diaz s/n
☎ 928 22 23 33 🕐 Daily
8–7 🚌 44, 45, 46 from Santa
Catalina 💷 Expensive

PUEBLO CANARIO

If you would like to see
some traditional dancing
check out the Canarian
Village. The dancing is
the result of a blend of
several different cultures
that left their influence
on the island–Spanish,
Portuguese and Latin
American. Traditional
accompanying music
sets the scene.
➕ b3 ✉ Parque
Doramas ☎ 928 24 35
93 🕐 Performances Sun
11.30am 🚌 1, 12, 13

QUETAL

This new bar is in the up-
and-coming nightlife area
of Calle Pelota, where

bars and restaurants are
buzzing. Chill out in white
plastic bucket seats with
pink fluffy cushions or
check out the clientele
from the upstairs balcony.
➕ c5 ✉ Calle Pelota 16
☎ 928 33 49 17 🕐 Daily
until 2am 🚌 1, 2, 3, 13

TEATRO CUYÁS

www.teatrocuyas.com
Opened in 2002 in
a former cinema, this
theatre hosts a range of
entertainment. You can
opt for modern drama,
ballet and classical music,
opera or comedy. Check
the local press for what's
on. Musicals are particu-
larly popular.
➕ c4 ✉ Calle Viera y Clavijo
s/n ☎ 928 43 21 80 🚌 2,
3, 8, 82, 83, 84

CINEMA

The biggest cinemas are all
in shopping malls. The latest
mainstream releases (often
dubbed) are screened at
Las Arenas (Multicines Las
Arenas ☎ 928 26 16 00),
La Ballena (Multicines La
Ballena ☎ 928 42 03 35)
and the El Muelle (Cinesa
☎ 902 33 32 31, www.cine-
sa.es) shopping complexes.
Options in the centre of town
are the Royal (Multcines
Royal, Calle León y Castillo
40 ☎ 928 36 09 54) and the
Monopol (Plaza de Hurtado
de Mendoza ☎ 928 36 74
38) in the student quarter.
Full listings can be found in
the local newspapers.

TEATRO PÉREZ GALDÓS

www.teatroperezgaldos.es
Opened after heavy
restoration work, this theatre is once again home
to the island's symphony
orchestra. It also hosts
opera–in particular
the distinctive Spanish
light opera known as
zarzuela–and ballet.
➕ c5 ✉ Plaza Stagno 1
☎ 928 43 38 05 🚌 1, 13

TERRAZA LA MARINA

The comfortably furnished
terrace can be found
to the rear of the Hotel
Reina Isabel, which leads
to the promenade and
to Las Canteras beach.
Perfectly placed for
watching people strolling
along at any time of day,
but particularly pleasant
on a warm evening.
➕ a1 ✉ Hotel Reina Isabel,
Calle Alfredo L Jones 40
☎ 928 26 01 00 🕐 Daily
10.30am–midnight 🚌 1, 3

UNIO DEPORTIVA DE LAS PALMAS

www.udlaspalmas.es
Gran Canaria's premier
football team play host to
other island and Spanish
teams, including local
rivals Tenerife. In 2008
the team was playing
for the Segunda División
A, Spain's second tier.
Matches take place at a
32,500-seat stadium.
➕ a3 ✉ Estadio de Gran
Canaria, Calle Pio XII 29
☎ 928 24 13 42 or 928 41 69
45; call for details of matches
🚌 2, 3, 20, 22, 25

Restaurants

PRICES

Prices are approximate, based on a 3-course meal for one person.

€€€	over €24
€€	€12–€24
€	under €12

EL ACUEDUCTO (€€–€€€)

All manner of meats is served in this comfortable, wood-beamed restaurant. Choose from steaks in every kind of sauce or roast leg of lamb, rounded off with desserts such as Catalan cream or fresh papaya.

➕ a1 ✉ Calle Sargento Llagas 45 ☎ 928 26 42 42 🕐 Lunch, dinner 🚌 1, 3, 41

AL MACCARONI (€€)

This friendly restaurant on the promenade has two dining areas, one less formal like a pizzeria, the other more formal but cozy and romantic with candles, dark red cloths and posing cherubs. Pizza, pasta and grills are on offer; try the piping hot baked macaroni cheese with bacon and peas in a terracotta dish.

➕ a1 ✉ Paseo de las Canteras 12 ☎ 928 27 15 80 🕐 Lunch, dinner 🚌 1, 12, 13, 41, 47

LA BUENA VIDA (€€)

The Good Life restaurant, near Vegueta market, is a welcome addition to the Las Palmas eating scene.

The design is modern and the menu creative. The chef, Toni Cavanillas, uses seasonal produce and changes the menu every three months. Booking is advised.

➕ c5 ✉ Calle Mendizábel 24 ☎ 928 33 58 64 🕐 Mon–Sat 1–4, 8.30–12.30 🚌 1, 9, 12, 13

CAFÉ MADRID (€)

A great atmosphere out on the pavement in front of the historic Hotel Madrid. Try the *menu del día* for good cooking and great value. The fun owners will ensure you will enjoy your meal.

➕ c5 ✉ Plaza de Cairasco 2 ☎ 928 36 06 64 🕐 Lunch, dinner 🚌 2, 3, 30, 90

CAFÉ SANTA CATALINA (€)

This café, established in 1959, is a set among the

CARNIVORES

There is a great tradition of meat eating in Gran Canaria and although vegetarians are now better catered for there are a plethora of restaurants serving grills and meat-related dishes. Beef (*carne de vacca*) is flown in from South America, in particular Argentina and Uruguay. Locally produced meat includes pork (*cerdo*), lamb (*cordro*) and kid (*cabrito*). Rabbit (*conejo*) is most often served in stews with a tasty savoury sauce.

trees and bougainvillea. In the background local men play chess, dominoes and cards; it is very much a locals' meeting place. Good coffee and light snacks— spaghetti, baguettes and salads.

➕ a1 ✉ Parque Santa Catalina 🕐 Daily 9am– midnight/1am 🚌 1, 2, 3 and all buses to Santa Catalina bus station

CAÑAS Y TAPAS (€)

Part of a chain, this café can be found on the busy Plaza de España and is a good place to pause from shopping in the nearby Avenida Mesa y López. Sip your coffee or nibble on a typical tapas lunch while people watching.

➕ a2 ✉ Plaza de España 5 ☎ 928 27 28 85 🕐 Daily 8am–midnight 🚌 3, 30, 44, 45, 46 47

CANDOMBE (€€)

Brazilian restaurant that specializes in skewered meat served with style at your table. All you can eat for a set price plus salads and garnishes. Doesn't include desserts or drinks.

➕ a1 ✉ Calle Sargento Llagas 43 ☎ 928 27 05 65 🕐 Lunch, dinner 🚌 1, 3, 41

CASA CARMELO (€€€)

The first-class grilled meat here is sourced from Argentina and Uruguay. If you take along a vegetarian or pescatarian there are copious amounts of salad on offer, and fish,

too. If it's chilly, there is an attractive indoor seating area, decked out Canarian style.

🔁 Off map at a1 ✉ Paseo de la Canteras 2 ☎ 928 46 90 56 🕓 Lunch, dinner 🚌 1, 20, 41, 47

CASA FATAGA (€€€)
www.casafataga.es
This charming restaurant in a tiny Canarian house is close to the Museo Elder. Sit outside among the flowers on the delightful arched terrace or sit indoors for the ambience of a Canarian home. They pride themselves on their wine list and their cheeses.

🔁 a1 ✉ Parque Santa Catalina ☎ 928 17 09 36 🕓 Lunch, dinner; closed Mon 🚌 1, 2, 3 and all buses to Santa Catalina bus station

CASA MONTESDEOCA (€€€)
www.casamontesdeoca.com
This gorgeous old house in the Vegueta quarter, built in the 16th century, houses one of Las Palmas's most elegant restaurants. Try to get a table on the patio beneath the trees. The service is formal and the food well presented.

🔁 c5 ✉ Calle Montesdeoca 10 ☎ 928 33 34 66 🕓 Lunch, dinner; closed Sun 🚌 1, 2, 3, 9, 12, 13

LA CAVA TRIANA (€–€€)
The entrance is up steps flanked by two straw

trees. Stylish décor with maroon walls hung with engravings, plus wooden tables and chairs and pendulous lighting. A strictly Spanish menu features meat main courses, tapas and a good selection of Spanish wines.

🔁 c5 ✉ Calle Travieso 35 ☎ 928 38 13 02 🕓 Lunch, dinner; closed Sun 🚌 3, 30, 82, 83, 84, 90

LOS CEDROS (€–€€)
A few minutes' walk behind the beach, this Lebanese restaurant has dark wood furniture, flowery tablecloths, ceramic floor tiles and pictures of Beirut and Lebanon on the walls. The menu reflects the country–chicken Lebanese-style, *ensalada Lebanesa*, cous cous, falafel and a variety of rice dishes.

🔁 a1 ✉ Calle Martínez de Escobar 68 ☎ 928 26 96 67 🕓 Lunch, dinner; closed Mon 🚌 1, 3, 12, 41

CANARIAN BEER
Beer is more popular than wine to drink with food in Gran Canaria, although the local wine is improving. The major island beer brand is Tropical, sold in bottles or on draught. Dorada from Tenerife is also a favourite. Most bars also stock international brands. A small glass of beer is a *caña*.

EL CERDO QUE RIE (€)
Although The Laughing Pig is located right on the promenade, it is reached down steps as if going into a cellar. Nice ambience with stone walls embellished with swords, striped tablecloths and rustic seating. Specialties of the house include grilled langoustines, Swedish salmon, peppered steaks and Chinese fondue. Round off with raspberry flambé or crêpes Suzette.

🔁 a1 ✉ Paseo de la Canteras 31 ☎ 928 26 36 49 🕓 Lunch, dinner 🚌 1, 3, 41

GALIA (€€€)
Go upmarket and French one night at this smart venue behind the beach. The pink and maroon, dimly lit romantic setting complements the delectable French cuisine.

🔁 a1 ✉ Calle Luis Morote 49 ☎ 928 22 32 19 🕓 Lunch, dinner; closed Sun 🚌 1, 3, 41

EL HERREÑO (€–€€)
Rustic venue close to the market. Great for traditional Canarian cooking washed down with local wine. Try the tasty roast pork and potatoes.

🔁 c5 ✉ Calle Mendizábal 5 ☎ 928 31 05 13 🕓 Lunch, dinner 🚌 1, 9, 12, 13

HOYA LA VIEJA (€€)
Taste some authentic Canarian home cooking

in this quaint small restaurant that displays old recipes and objects in the window. You can sit out on the cobbled pavement or eat in the small indoor restaurant.

🚹 c4 ✉ Calle Perdomo 15 ☎ 928 36 04 60 🕒 Lunch, dinner 🚌 8, 82, 83, 84, 91

LOOPY'S (€€)

One of the smarter promside restaurants with an upstairs outdoor terrace. Inside you are greeted with lots of wood and a nautical theme. There's a big menu—the salads are particularly good—with grills, fish and the specialty here, Loopy's famous pizzas.

🚹 a1 ✉ Paseo de las Canteras 30 ☎ 928 27 62 49 🕒 Lunch, dinner 🚌 1, 12, 13, 41, 47

LA MARINERA (€€–€€€)

In the northern area of the beach known as La Puntilla, this restaurant has excellent sea views, especially from the terrace at sunset. Primarily a seafood and fish restaurant, it also offers tender grilled meats. Try the seafood paella.

🚹 Off map at a1 ✉ Calle Alonso Ojeda ☎ 928 46 88 02 🕒 Lunch, dinner 🚌 1, 20, 41, 47

EL NOVILLO PRECOZ (€€€)

www.novilloprecoz.com
Beef is flown in from Uruguay three times a

week at this upmarket grill that boasts 10 different types of steak dishes. Once inside you'll find a warm atmosphere enhanced by the open grill. The walls are covered with photographs, some incongruously of once-living cattle. Vegetarians stay away.

🚹 a1 ✉ Calle Portugal 9 ☎ 928 26 54 02 🕒 Lunch, dinner; closed Mon 🚌 45, 47

LA PASTA REAL (€)

This restaurant, one of the few dedicated to vegetarians, looks a bit scruffy from the outside but beyond the façade is a quaint, family-run business with lace tablecloths and rough stone walls. A good standard of pastas, pizzas and salads.

🚹 a2 ✉ Calle Secretario Padilla 28 ☎ 928 26 22 67

LAS PALMAS INTERNATIONAL

International cuisine is only just beginning to make an impact on the city and there are still many restaurants cooking authentic Canarian. The Italian influence is probably the most long standing and you will find many authentic pizza and pasta restaurants along the seafront and down in the old town. If you look below the surface, you can find grills from Brazil, falafel from Lebanon and cordon bleu from France.

🕒 Lunch, dinner; closed Tue 🚌 1, 3, 41

LA PIZZA (€–€€)

Cheerful place with red-and-white checked cloths and a trickling water feature. It's not just pizza but pasta, meat and fish, too.

🚹 a1 ✉ Calle Tomás Miller 64 ☎ 928 26 85 79 🕒 Lunch, dinner 🚌 1, 3, 45, 47

RESTAURANTE ROMA (€–€€)

Maybe you don't come to Gran Canaria to eat Italian food but this is a good option, especially as the sea views are so good. The décor is Roman, with murals of the Colosseum and Trevi Fountain to accompany your meal. Eat pizza and pasta on the terrace or balcony.

🚹 Off map at a1 ✉ Paseo de la Canteras 1 ☎ 928 48 61 12 🕒 Lunch, dinner 🚌 1, 20, 41, 47

TEA AND COFFEE POT (€)

Take a break after a visit to the market in Vegueta at this trendy modern café that attracts locals and students from the nearby university. It's a good place to people-watch and serves some interesting fresh juices and a range of coffees, teas and snacks.

🚹 c5 ✉ Calle Mendizábal 20 ☎ 928 32 19 66 🕒 Daily early to late 🚌 1, 9, 12, 13

At first glance the south seems to consist of concrete cities in a barren landscape where the majority of visitors come for the sunshine and beautiful beaches. But you don't have to travel far from the mass tourism to catch a glimpse of dramatic scenery, quaint villages and rural life.

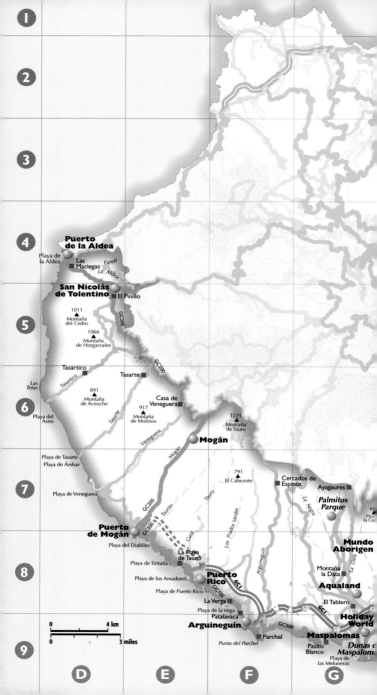

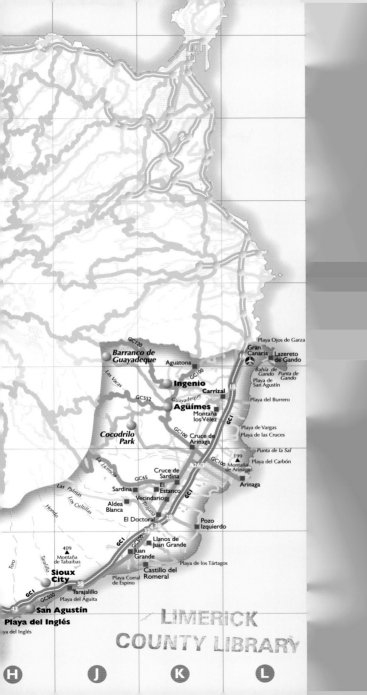

Playa Ojos de Garza

Gran
Canaria   Lazereto
de Gando

*Bahía de
Gando*   *Punta de
Gando*
Playa de
San Agustín

GC120

*Barranco de
Guayadeque*
Aguatona

GC100

Ingenio
Carrizal

18

Playa del Burrero

GC552
Guayadeque
Agüimes
Montaña
los Vélez

Las Vacas

Playa de Vargas
Playa de las Cruces

GC100   Cruce de
Arinaga

GC1

*Cocodrilo
Park*

Punta de la Sal
Playa del Carbón

GC100   260   199   Montaña
de Arinaga

La Licencia

Cruce de
Sardina

Las Palmas   GC65

Los Cultillas   Sardina   El
Estanco   Arinaga

Hondo   Vecindario

Aldea
Blanca

Timpima   GC1

El Doctoral
28

Pozo
Izquierdo

32 30

Toro   GC1

GC500   Llanos de
Juan Grande

409
Montaña
de Tabaibas   Juan
Grande

Tarajalillo

Castillo del
Romeral

Playa de los Tártagos

**Sioux
City**
38
Tarajalillo
Playa del Águita

Playa Corral
de Espino

GC1
GC300   **San Agustín**
43
Playa del Inglés

ya del Inglés

LIMERICK
COUNTY LIBRARY

H   **J**   **K**   **L**

Barranco de Guayadeque

TOP 25

HIGHLIGHTS

- Old town of Agüimes
- Information centre
- Cave restaurants
- Guanche settlements
- Views from GC120 at Ingenio

TIP

- Where the road runs out at Tagoror, it is possible to continue on foot along a magnificent route, but this should only be attempted by experienced walkers with a good map or guide.

On the eastern side of the island lies a spectacular canyon where the spiritual descendants of the Guanches live in caves as their ancestors did in pre-Spanish times.

Natural wonder Carving relentlessly through the landscape, the gorge twists and turns to the coast, via Ingenio and Agüimes. The walls of the ravine rise out from the dry river bed, through lush green terraces, tall palms, eucalyptus and prickly pear, to lofty crags of red volcanic rock, characteristics typical of Gran Canaria but at their most remarkable here. The entire gorge has been designated a nature reserve. A paradise for lovers of botany, this great natural space shelters some 80 native species of flora, including many of the island's rarest plants.

Clockwise from far left: The way into the barranco; crops are grown in terraces up the gorge's steep sides; cave houses in the rock face; more modern dwellings built against the rock wall; local farmers

Cultural heritage Apart from its great natural beauty, the *barranco* is one of the island's most fascinating archaeological sites. The aboriginal inhabitants who once lived in this fertile land left behind both natural and man-made caves that serve various purposes. Burial chambers found here form an important part of the Guanche exhibits of the Museo Canario in Las Palmas (▶ 27). The area is little populated today, but most of those who remain still farm the land, keep animals and live in cave dwellings. Restaurants, like the popular Tagoror (▶ 70), have been set up in some of these caves. A visit to the Centro de Interpretación de Guayadeque, in a cave network near Agüimes, will tell you more about the *barranco's* fascinating inhabitants and show you how to build a cave home. There is also information on the gorge's agriculture and flora.

THE BASICS

➕ J5
✉ Signposted from GC100, Municipality of Agüimes
🕐 Centro de Interpretación Tue–Sat 9–5, Sun 10–6
🍴 Restaurants/cafés and picnic/barbecue areas along the route
🚌 41, 52 to Agüimes from Maspalomas
♿ Centro de Interpretación inexpensive
❓ Maps marking footpaths are available from the information centre

Dunas de Maspalomas

TOP
25

HIGHLIGHTS

● Birding
● Walking barefoot across the dunes
● Camel ride
● Sand formations

TIPS

● If you walk across the dunes, take plenty of water and avoid the heat of the day.
● Don't stray from the designated route.
● Don't feed the fish in the lagoon—they eat the mosquito larvae.

Made up of three very different ecosystems—the rolling dunes, the former palm grove and a coastal lagoon—this magical and surreal landscape is an area of natural beauty and ecological importance.

Life in the desert Dividing Maspalomas beach from Playa del Inglés at the southernmost tip of the island, these undulating dunes are composed of fine ground shells that can reach a height of 10m (33ft) and are spread over an area of 404ha (998 acres). Created by a combination of sea and wind, the dunes resemble a host of contoured hillocks and valleys. The area is a paradise for nudists, who sunbathe in the *borjanas,* slits resembling half-moons eroded by the wind. You might also encounter a camel train loaded with tourists trekking through the terrain.

Clockwise from left: Vista of shifting sand dunes; the freshwater lagoon is a haven for seabirds; the sand dunes with the mountainous interior in the background; bird footprints in the sand

La Charca Classified as a Special Nature Reserve, this seawater and freshwater lagoon and its palm grove, sitting behind the beach, is home to over 20 different species of birds, and there are signs that the lagoon is being used increasingly as a stopping point by many migrating birds.

Environmental virtue In recent years, ecologists have been voicing their concerns about the mass construction that is encroaching on the area. Local authorities are taking steps to protect the region from further depredation and have plans to reintroduce plant and bird species that were once a common sight in the reserve. You can gain access to the dunes via a designated path that leads from the small information office at the Rui Grand Palace Maspalomas hotel (▷ 112), which has an exhibition on their history and ecology.

THE BASICS

➕ H9

✉ Maspalomas, 6km (4 miles) south of Playa del Inglés

🕐 Information centre daily but hours are erratic

🍴 Plenty of choices on and beside the beach

🚌 Numerous services from all areas to Faro de Maspalomas bus terminal; 30 from Las Palmas

❓ You may see the occasional nudist or witness gay cruising

Maspalomas

Maspalomas light-house (left); El Oasis beach (middle); typical apartments (right)

THE BASICS

G9

6km (4 miles) south-west of Playa del Inglés; 58km (36 miles) south of Las Palmas

Many cafés and restaurants

Numerous services from all areas to Faro de Maspalomas bus terminal; 30 from Las Palmas

HIGHLIGHTS

● Sand dunes (▷ 50–51)
● Golf
● El Faro shopping centre (▷ 64)
● Strolling along the promenade

Until the 1960s only a solitary lighthouse stood at this southernmost point, then the first plans for tourist development began, starting the battle for the dunes.

The resort With its upmarket image, magnificent sand dunes and luxury hotels built around the oasis, Maspalomas resembles something out of a film set. But as you venture back from the seafront you will discover a well-concealed urbanization of low-rise select apartments, which soon gives way to denser tourist accommodation. The 18-hole Campo de Golf separates most of this sprawl from the beach area, and wide avenues, named after the tour operators who brought such prosperity to the region, divide it into sections. Amusement parks border the resort's northern edge.

The coastline A 55m (180ft) lighthouse marks the western boundary along the coastline, behind which sit the dunes of Maspalomas (▷ 50–51) and the lagoon. To the east it merges into the developing resort of Meloneras. Between these two points is a chic promenade lined with equally chic shopping centres, bars, restaurants and luxury hotels.

Sun, sea and sand The main draw is sunbath-ing on the Blue Flag beach and swimming in the clear waters of the Atlantic Ocean. When the sun sets many enjoy a gentle stroll along the prom-enade, and late into the evening like to try their luck at the casino (▷ 66). For the more energetic, golf is fast becoming a number one attraction and there are numerous opportunities for watersports.

Mundo Aborigen

If you are intrigued by Gran Canaria's pre-Hispanic culture a visit to this museum, dedicated to a world lost in the 15th century, will satisfy your curiosity.

Earliest inhabitants This cultural theme park is based on the chronicles of the first Spanish conquistadors, who found the ancient Canarian people living in well-organized, close-knit communities making use of the resources the environment offered. The people are invariably described as gentle and kind, lovers of sport and music yet redoubtable in battle.

The spirit of the Guanches The open-air museum recreates a Stone Age settlement spread across the upper hillsides of the Barranco de Fataga. Follow the trail around the carefully planned itinerary for an insight into the different aspects of Guanche life. A series of tableaux and scale models, some of them rather graphic, complete with reproductions of stone houses and burial caves, bring the story to life. Vivid descriptions in Spanish, English and German give an informative account about everything from milling flour, cooking and craft skills to surgery, religious ceremonies, social hierarchy, magic and social customs.

Spectacular views The pre-Hispanic culture of Gran Canaria is strongly evoked on this lovely hillside and the views back towards the coast. To the west, dark gorges recede into the distance, and to the south looms the resort of Playa del Inglés and the Maspalomas dunes.

THE BASICS

www.mundoaborigen.com

➕ H8

✉ GC60 (Carretera Playa del Inglés–Fataga, km 6)

☎ 928 17 22 95

🕐 Daily 9–6

💰 Expensive

🍴 Café on premises

🚌 18 from Maspalomas

♿ Few

HIGHLIGHTS

- Pre-Hispanic culture
- Nobleman's house
- Council chamber
- Views over the canyon

Palmitos Parque

TOP 25

Exotic blooms and cacti thrive (left and middle); visitors strolling (right)

THE BASICS

www.palmitospark.es

🔲 G7

✉ Barranco de los Palmitos, 15km (9 miles) northwest of Playa del Inglés

☎ 928 79 70 70

🕐 Daily 10–6

💰 Expensive

🍴 Café/refreshments in park

🚍 45 or 451 from Playa del Inglés or San Agustín; 70 or 701 from Puerto Rico

♿ Good

❓ Parrot show 10.30, 11.30, 2.30, 3.30, 4.30; birds of prey show 12.15, 2; exotic bird exhibition 1

HIGHLIGHTS

● Colourful hummingbirds
● Birds of prey show
● Tropical aquarium
● Parrot show
● Primates Island
● Exotic bird exhibition

Exotic birds flourish in a lush valley of palm trees at this subtropical park in a wonderful mountain valley at the head of the Barranco de Chamoriscán.

Birds galore With more than 200 species of birds, including toucans, peacocks, flamingos, birds of prey and tiny hummingbirds, the park manages to strike a good balance between education, conservation and entertainment. Children will love the parrot show; the willing performers have been trained to do amazing tricks, such as constructing jigsaws or riding a bike, to rapturous applause.

Other attractions Originally opened in the 1970s, the park endeavours to improve facilities. Additional attractions include a large aquarium where tropical fish from the Pacific and the Amazon swim in a natural and dramatic setting. There is a cactus garden with diverse cacti and aloe plants, a butterfly house with inhabitants from all over the world, and a spectacular orchid house. More recent housemates include reptiles, small mammals and two white gibbons and three orang-utans that reside on Primates Island.

Take a break Winding paths lead you from one attraction to the next, past a stream, through palm groves and giant euphorbia. Cafés and ice-cream kiosks are scattered throughout the park and you are welcome to take your own picnic. At the end of your visit you can buy a memento at the souvenir shop—perhaps a stuffed toy parrot—or have your photo taken with a screeching macaw.

TOP 25

Playa del Inglés

If only out of curiosity, you should visit this brash concrete conurbation to see why it has become a symbol of the prosperity tourism brought to Gran Canaria.

Costa Canaria What were formerly no more than barren tomato fields have been transformed into what some would describe as a soulless place. Don't expect authentic Spanish life, a historic old quarter or charming plaza with shady trees. Instead, you are likely to get lost among identical wide boulevards with identical high-rise hotels. Life focuses on commercial centres, such as the Yumbo Centrum (▷ 65), containing a warren of small shops, bars, restaurants and entertainment.

Fun, fun, fun So what is it that brings the holidaymakers flocking to Playa? The resort is a non-stop holiday playground, with accommodation, restaurants and nightlife to suit all tastes, and excellent public transport. The long coastal promenade, Paseo Costa Canaria, looks out over the vast Blue Flag beach of fine sand, where every facility is on hand, including watersports, sunbeds and parasols. At sunset the promenade, which runs from San Agustín to the Dunes de Maspalomas (▷ 50–51), makes for an enjoyable stroll.

Facelift In order to dispel some of the negative hype, much of the accommodation has been refurbished and the resort has started to get a much-needed makeover. Lots of money has been spent on planting lush and colourful foliage, which helps to disguise the concrete.

THE BASICS

✚ H9
✉ 6km (4 miles) northwest of Maspalomas; 52km (32 miles) south of Las Palmas
🍴 Many options
🚌 30 from Las Palmas; many local buses

HIGHLIGHTS

● Paseo Costa Canario
● The beach
● Watersports
● View from the Hotel Riu Palace *mirador* at sunset over sand dunes
● Nightlife

Puerto de Mogán

HIGHLIGHTS

● Fish restaurants
● Views from El Faro
● Picturesque marina
● Shallow water for swimming
● Old village quarter

TIPS

● From the cliffs at the western end of the port there's a fine view of the sun setting.
● Whales and dolphins are a common sight in these waters; the best way to spot them is to take a boat trip.

Simply a fishing village until the 1980s, this seafaring town of singular beauty lives up to its reputation as the perfect example of tourist development that does not violate the natural landscape.

As pretty as a picture Low-rise pueblo-style apartments with painted borders, hibiscus hedges and roof gardens covered with bougainvillea are the ideal backdrops for the marina. Sometimes referred to as 'Little Venice', Venetian-style bridges arching over canals enhance the picturesque setting. Wandering around the waterside admiring luxury yachts, and stopping for refreshment and people watching in a waterfront café, is an idyllic way to pass time. A stroll out to the El Faro restaurant (▷ 69) at the end of the harbour is rewarded with amazing panoramic views of the resort. The

Clockwise from left: Puerto de Mogán is known for its attractive architecture; boats in the marina; alfresco dining at the Pescador restaurant; view of the marina with the lighthouse in the background

harbour is a fabulous place to sample local sea-food at one of the many excellent restaurants. Boat trips and fishing and diving excursions leave from the harbour, including the Yellow Submarine (▷ 67), and a glass-bottom boat ferries visitors along the coast to Puerto Rico and Arguineguín.

The beach A small beach of golden sand forms an arc around the clear warm waters, which are protected by a breakwater and are ideal for safe bathing. Behind the beach is a traffic-free prom-enade, lined with cafés and restaurants. Back from here upmarket shops and luxury hotels and apartments are gradually filling the space, beyond which the mountains loom dramatically in the background. For a sharp contrast with the port, climb the narrow, stepped streets of the authentic old town clinging to the cliffs above.

THE BASICS

➕ E8

✉ 29km (17 miles) north-west of Playa del Inglés

🍴 Many options

🚌 1 from Las Palmas; 32 from Playa del Inglés

⛴ Lineas Salmon boat to Puerto Rico, Arguineguín (www.lineassalmon.com)

More to See

AGÜIMES

www.aguimes.es

This thriving town retains a strong Canarian identity through its arts and crafts tradition. Workshops produce open-weave cloth, stone articles, ceramics, traditional costumes, and lots more. Strolling through the old town is a delight. St. Sebastián Church has a neoclassical façade that is one of the best architectural examples in the Canary Islands. Plaza de San Antón, the focus for different festivities organized year round, houses the Agüimes interpretation centre, a must-see for visitors interested in the town's natural surroundings. Come in the winter months and see the volcanic landscape transformed by flowering plants and lush vegetation.

🚩 K6 ✉ 29km (17 miles) northeast of Playa del Inglés 📷 Centro de Interpretación 928 12 41 83 🍴 Bars and cafés 🚌 41 from Maspalomas

ARGUINEGUÍN

Don't be deterred by the cement factory on the outskirts, and the increasing development either side, as once at the heart of this working fishing town you will begin to appreciate the bustling atmosphere. The biggest draw is the excellent fish restaurants serving the catch of the day, and the town is particularly popular on Tuesday and Thursday when it hosts one of the area's biggest markets. You can take a walk west along the coastal promenade to Patalavaca and the luxury club resort of Anfi del Mar, created by a Norwegian entrepreneur in 1988, with its beach of imported Caribbean sand.

🚩 F9 ✉ 14km (9 miles) west of Playa del Inglés 🍴 Several restaurants 🚌 32 from Playa del Inglés

AQUALAND

www.aqualand.es

An action-packed world of water with over 29 rides and thrills has something for all. The vertiginous speed of the Kamikaze is a pure adrenalin rush; family favourite Mamut is a waterslide aboard a four-person raft; float down the Congo River if you're

Whitewashed buildings of Agüimes

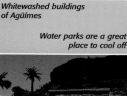

Water parks are a great place to cool off

feeling lazy; while Mini Park caters for the very young.

✚ G8 ✉ Carretera Palmitos Park, km 3 ☎ 928 14 05 25 🕐 Daily 10–5 (closed in bad weather) 🍴 Various options 🚌 701 from Maspalomas; 451 from Playa del Inglés ♿ Park good; no access to slides 💵 Expensive

COCODRILO PARK

This private concern run by the Balser family started life in 1988 as a rescue centre for crocodiles. The range of rescued animals has grown considerably, and as well as over 300 crocodiles, inmates now include turtles, monkeys, deer, tigers, llamas and pigs, among many others. Funds received by opening to the public assist with the upkeep of the animals and the park.

✚ J6 ✉ Carretera General Los Corralillos, km 5, Villa de Agüimes ☎ 928 78 47 25 🕐 Sun–Fri 10–6 ♿ Good 💵 Moderate

HOLIDAY WORLD

www.holidayworld-maspalomas.com
In addition to a funfair, Holiday World has a wealth of other entertainment:

bowling, a leisure centre, a nightclub, pubs and restaurants are just some of the attractions you will find at this, the biggest amusement park in the Canary Islands.

✚ H9 ✉ Avevida Touroperador Tui, Maspalomas ☎ 928 73 04 98 🕐 Park daily 6–midnight (shorter hours in winter); bowling Sun–Thu 10am–2am, Fri 10am–3am, Sat 10am–4am 🍴 Various options 🚌 25, 30, 45, 70 from Maspalomas ♿ Good 💵 Free; charge for individual attractions

INGENIO

Visit the real Gran Canaria and meet real Canarians at this expanding town known for its traditional handicrafts. Stop by the Museo de Piedra y Artesanía (▷ 65) to see the skilled artisans at work. The name Ingenio means 'sugarmill', and sugar production was important to the early development of the town, although it is no longer grown in any quantity. Start to explore the narrow winding streets of the old centre at Plaza de la Candelaria, which is dominated by the church dating from 1901.

THE SOUTH

★

MORE TO SEE

Museo de Piedra y Artesanía, Ingenio

Carved wooden balcony, Mogán

✚ K6 ✉ 31km (19 miles) northeast of Playa del Inglés 🍴 Restaurants/cafés in town 🚌 41 from Maspalomas

MOGÁN

Inland from Puerto de Mogán, the road gently climbs the *barranco* through a tropical valley of mangoes, avocados and papaya, to the sleepy white town of Mogán. Here you can still sample a rural lifestyle—rustic houses line the narrow roads, with terracotta pots littering the roadside.

✚ E6 ✉ 37km (23 miles) northwest of Playa del Inglés 🍴 Restaurants/cafés in town 🚌 84 from Puerto de Mogán

PUERTO DE LA ALDEA

Sheltering beneath a mountainous cape, this little harbour town has a small pebble beach and excellent fish restaurants along the promenade: This is one of the best places on the island to watch the sunset (but be prepared—it can get very windy). Behind, among a pine wood, is a picnic area. The freshwater pond (*charco*), is the setting for the Fiesta del Charco in September, when excited locals are found leaping and splashing in the *charco,* brandishing bunches of vegetation trying to catch fish with their bare hands.

✚ D4 ✉ 75km (46 miles) northwest of Playa del Inglés 🍴 Restaurants in town 🚌 38 from Puerto de Mogán

PUERTO RICO

Rows of white apartment blocks encircle Puerto Rico's crescent-shaped bay and continue to climb the steep hillside behind. The marinas on either side of the bay are crowded with offers of every conceivable water activity. Big-game fishing is popular off these shores, where barracuda, swordfish, shark and blue marlin are on the enthusiastic anglers wish list. A clifftop path separates Puerto Rico from fast developing Amadores, with its glorious manmade beach. Although rather over built, Puerto Rico is popular with British families.

✚ E8 ✉ 20km (12 miles) west of Playa del Inglés 🍴 Restaurants on the beach front and in town 🚌 32 from Playa del Inglés

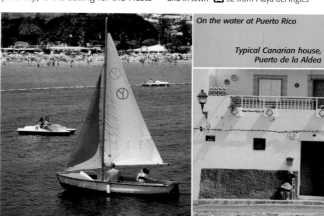

On the water at Puerto Rico

Typical Canarian house, Puerto de la Aldea

SAN AGUSTÍN

San Agustín is often referred to as 'Little Scandinavia', due to an increasing number of Scandinavians who are not only holidaying here, but also setting up home. Although on the doorstep of Playa del Inglés, the resort has escaped mass tourism and is much quieter than its neighbour. Consisting of mostly low-rise apartments with a scattering of 4-star hotels, it does tend to appeal to older people. A coastal path that leads all the way to Playa del Inglés edges two black-sand beaches.

🔁 H8 ✉ 4km (2.5 miles) northeast of Playa del Inglés 🍴 Restaurants on beach front and in town 🚌 32 from Playa del Inglés

SAN NICOLÁS DE TOLENTINO

In a broad and dusty valley, San Nicolás is mostly a residential town surrounded by slopes overgrown with tropical fruit, cacti and bamboo. At the heart is a beautiful church that features some interesting sculptural works created by Luján Pérez. Nearby,

Cactualdea is a nature park with over 1,200 species of cactus, as well as fountains, caves, a craft market and an amphitheatre where Canarian wrestling takes place.

🔁 D5 ✉ 20km (12 miles) west of Playa del Inglés 🕐 Cactualdea daily 10–6 🍴 Cafés in town 🚌 38 from Puerto de Mogán

SIOUX CITY

www.siouxcity-grancanaria.com
Come on down to this wild-west frontier town constructed in the remains of an old spaghetti-western film set, where productions such as *A Fistful of Dollars* were filmed. Actors in costume play the role of dancing saloon girls, cowboys, Indians and bandits. Be sure to catch one of the action-packed shows, which might include stunt riders, knife throwing, lassooing, and much more. Friday night is barbecue night.

🔁 H8 ✉ Barranco del Aguila, San Agustín ☎ 928 76 25 73 🕐 Tue–Sun 10–5 (also Fri 8pm–midnight) 🍴 Restaurant on site 🚌 29 from Playa del Inglés ♿ Good ✋ Expensive

Black sand beach at San Agustín

Winding up into the mountains from San Nicolás de Tolentino

San Agustín to Maspalomas

This walk follows the coast to Maspalomas lighthouse. There is no shade on the beach, so go early morning or evening.

DISTANCE: 8km (5 miles)   **ALLOW:** 2.5 hours

START

SAN AGUSTÍN
✚ H8 🚌 32 from Playa del Inglés

❶ Start from the grey sand beach at San Agustín (▷ 61) and, taking the seafront promenade to the right, pass hotel gardens at first, then apartments.

❷ Climbing a little above the rocks, the path circles around the beach of Las Burras, where fishing boats rest on the sands. The tall buildings of Playa del Inglés (▷ 55) are now firmly in view.

❸ Approaching along the promenade, ahead you will see a wooden footbridge. The café on the right-hand side of the bridge serves tasty *bocadillos* (filled bread rolls), salad and freshly squeezed fruit drinks.

❹ Passing the Europalace Hotel, the promenade ascends several flights of steps. At the top of the steps, go around the shopping centre to pick up the promenade again. It continues along the top of a modest cliff.

END

PLAYA DEL INGLÉS
✚ H9 🚌 32 to San Agustín

❽ About 20 minutes brings you to Maspalomas, passing the lagoon to the right. You might want to avert your eyes as the area is scattered with nude sunbathers. As you near Maspalomas, turn towards the sea and head for the lighthouse.

❼ In front, the golden Maspalomas dunes now rise, not in long ridges but in individual hillocks. Follow the fringe of beach around the dunes, and pick up one of the designated routes to cross the dunes. This is quite a hard trek so take plenty of water.

❻ Turn left along the road onto the now golden beach, then follow the beach to the right. Narrow at first, it soon expands, with beach beds, bars and, near the end, a nudist zone.

❺ At the centre of Playa del Inglés the promenade descends again across the only road along the route, Avenida de Alféreces Provisionales.

Shopping

LA BODEGUILLA JUANANÁ
This quirky shop sells authentic local products, including art, ceramic bowls, wine and cheeses, which are used or on display in their adjoining restaurant (▷ 68).
🔲 E8 ✉ Local 390, Harbour Puerto de Mogán ☎ 928 56 50 44

CANDLE PALACE
Whatever your candle requirements, you will find every colour, shape and size at this small waterside shop, where everything is made on the premises.
🔲 E8 ✉ Local 139, Harbour Puerto de Mogán ☎ 928 72 52 01

CENTRO COMERCIAL BELLAVISTA
A light and airy shopping complex with a domed glass roof and palm trees. Plenty of small shops, not high-street names but intimate boutiques selling everything from fashion and sportswear to jewellery, shoes and toys.
🔲 G9 ✉ Calle Partera Leonorita 22, San Fernando, Maspalomas ☎ 928 77 63 89

CENTRO COMMERCIAL CITA
www.cc-cita.com
Maybe a little ragged around the edges, but the exterior of this shopping centre still makes visitors stop and look. Like something out of a children's pop-up book, it is

decorated with vast replicas of world landmarks.
🔲 H9 ✉ Avenida de Francia, Playa del Inglés ☎ 928 76 28 43

CENTRO COMERCIAL FARO 2
www.faro2.es
A striking abstract feature rises up from the centre of this circular mall that is surrounded by lush gardens. The contemporary spiral theme continues inside, where you will find a variety of shops, restaurants and cafés.
🔲 G9 ✉ Plaza Touroperador Holland International, Campo Internacional de Maspalomas ☎ 928 76 91 97

CENTRO COMERCIAL SAN AGUSTÍN
Moroccan bazaar-type layout, where among the

PROMENADE SHOPPING
Shop till you drop at Maspalomas without even leaving the seafront. The promenade that stretches from the *faro* through to Meloneras leads past a parade of shopping malls offering all types of retail therapy. The newest of these is El Faro Boulevard, two low-rise octagonal buildings linked by a large water feature, which boasts designer shops and individual boutiques aimed at the clientele hanging out at the neighbouring 5-star hotels.

usual kitsch souvenirs are some genuine artisan items. The open-air top floor has views out to sea, and there is a fitness centre and children's amusements.
🔲 H8 ✉ Calle de las Dalías, San Agustín

EARTH COLLECTION
www.theearthcollection.com
Environmentally friendly clothing, in distinctive individual designs for men and women, made of a combination of organic silk and cotton. The shop carries the slogan 'make a difference buy green'.
🔲 E8 ✉ Local 103, Harbour Puerto de Mogán ☎ 928 56 50 58

FEDAC
www.fedac.org
FEDAC's aim is to maintain and develop traditional Canarian crafts; at this outlet, which is attached to the tourist information office, they sell all manner of items guaranteed to be genuine Canarian craftsmanship.
🔲 H9 ✉ Centro Insular de Turismo, Avenida de España/ Avenida de los Estados Unidos, Playa del Inglés ☎ 928 77 24 45

FUND GRUBE
www.fundgrube.es
This chain store has branches throughout the Canary Islands, and this large circular outlet on the seafront stocks

sunglasses, handbags, watches perfume, alcohol and tobacco, all at tax-free prices.

⊞ G9 ⊠ Local 33 Varadero, Paseo Meloneras, Maspalomas ☎ 928 14 34 10

LA GALERÍA

The range of island handicrafts stocked at this gift shop is a step up from items sold at other bazaar-type shops in the Yumbo Centre. You may even uncover the occasional hidden gem.

⊞ H9 ⊠ Local 231-07 2nd floor, Yumbo Centre, Playa del Inglés ☎ 928 76 99 68

GRIMALDI

Grimaldi has been offering the finest jewellery on Gran Canaria for over 12 years. All that glitters here is truly gold—everything is 18-carat gold, and comes with certification and warranty for complete assurance. There is something to suit every wallet, and the German staff provide an individual service.

⊞ H9 ⊠ 1st floor CC CITA, Playa del Inglés ☎ 928 77 12 86

MACY'S SPORT

A designer name in the Yumbo centre is not a common occurrence. This chain store sells many of the top names, including Hugo Boss, Armani Jeans and Roberto Cavalli.

⊞ H9 ⊠ 2nd floor, Yumbo Centre, Playa del Inglés ☎ 928 77 07 27

MUSEO DE PIEDRA Y ARTESANIA CANARIA

The Canary Stone Craftwork Museum makes a good point of reference for those wishing to purchase arts and crafts made in local workshops: particularly ceramics, textiles and palm products and rocks.

⊞ K6 ⊠ Camino Real de Grande 1, Ingenio ☎ 928 78 11 24

PERLA CANARIA

www.perlacanaria.com
An extensive range of pearls and pearl jewellery is displayed in this outlet inside C.C. Faro 2. Quality cultured pearls are bought from exotic places such as Tahiti, Australia and Japan.

⊞ H8 ⊠ C.C. Faro 2, local B 241 ☎ 928 77 80 14

CENTROS COMERCIALES

Shopping can be a bizarre experience in the southern resorts because, with the exception of Puerto de Mogán, activity is concentrated in the huge concrete warrens called *centros comerciales*. Nobody will be surprised if you bargain over the prices quoted, so take the opportunity to haggle for items such as perfumes, leather goods, clothes and electronic products.

RINCON CANARIO

Among the more conventional souvenirs at this gift shop are some traditional locally made products, including *mojo* sauce, honey and rum liqueur (Guayaro).

⊞ E8 ⊠ Local 105, Harbour Puerto de Mogan

EL TROZITO

A new concept has come to San Fernando. Tasty and healthy Swedish pies, which look more like a quiche than a traditional pie, are baked on the premises by a mother and daughter team. The wide selection includes fillings such as broccoli with blue cheese and walnuts, prawns and spinach or salmon and dill.

⊞ H8 ⊠ Local 59, Centro Commercial San Fernando, Maspalomas ☎ 928 77 72 39

YUMBO CENTRUM

www.cc-yumbo.com
This huge warren of commercial enterprises is the biggest mall in Playa del Inglés. Divided into two parts by a central garden area, you will find banks, pharmacies, high-street names, restaurants, cafés and bars among all the usual tourist tat. At night, the centre is the main focus for the island's gay scene.

⊞ H9 ⊠ Avenida de los Estados Unidos 54, Playa del Inglés ☎ 928 76 41 96

Entertainment and Activities

BACHIRA

www.bachira.com

This smart club is in a basement setting and has three bars. DJs play mainstream dance music while slideshows are projected on the walls.

H9 ⊠ Avenida de Italia 27, Playa del Inglés ⏰ Thu–Sat midnight–late

CAMELLO SAFARI DUNAS

www.camellosafari.com

For something completely different join a fun camel safari across the sand dunes of Maspalomas. The circular tour takes half an hour to complete. Reservations essential.

H8 ⊠ Booking office Avenida Dunas Isla de Lobos 70, San Fernando ☎ 928 76 07 81 ⏰ Daily 9–4.30

CASINO TAMARINDOS

www.casinotamarindos.es

A full range of table games and slot machines, plus fine dining, for the serious gambler. You must be over 18, abide by the dress code and carry ID. Free admission.

H8 ⊠ Hotel Meliá Tamarindos, Calle Las Retamas 3, San Agustín ☎ 928 76 27 24 ⏰ Nightly 9pm–4am (shorter hours in winter)

CHIC/CREAM

www.chicmaspalomas.com

A 20-something crowd pack out this fashionable disco-club for the best party nights in town, while internationally famous DJs fill the large dance floor with house music.

G9 ⊠ Plaza de Maspalomas, Playa del Inglés ⏰ Nightly midnight–7am

CHINAWHITE… COSTA!

Top DJs spin R&B, hip-hop and current hits at this funky disco bar with stylish black and white leather stools and glass tables.

H9 ⊠ Top floor, CC Kasbah, Playa del Inglés ☎ 928 77 17 30 ⏰ Nightly 10pm–4am

CLUB COSTA GABANA

www.costagabana.es

A popular new addition, this chic bar has an orange and black theme running through the décor that fits well with the equally chic surroundings on the Maspalomas promenade. A glass-fronted terrace with patio heaters allows you enjoy a cocktail overlooking the sea. Live music.

G9 ⊠ El Boulevard Faro, Maspalomas ☎ 928 14 34 68 ⏰ Nightly 5pm–4am

CLUB MISTRAL

www.club-mistral.com

A team of professional instructors offer a complete programme of windsurfing instruction on every level. For the more experienced, there are excursions to high-wind spots further north and windsurf safaris. Also kitesurfing and surfboarding.

J8 ⊠ Carretera General del Sur km 47, Playa de Tarajalillo, Bahía Feliz ☎ 928 15 71 58 ⏰ Daily 9.30–5.30

DIVE ACADEMY

www.diveacademy-grancanaria.com

Multilingual instructors teach PADI diving courses to beginners and experienced divers. Day trips for certified divers are also available.

F9 ⊠ Club Amigos del Atlantico Calle La Lajilla, Arguineguín ☎ 928 73 61 96

DRAGO'S BOITE

Down in the depths of the Hotel Meliá Tamarindos, this sophisticated cave-like nightclub has bamboo features on the ceiling and

---

ANYONE FOR GOLF?

An ideal climate, varied landscape and proximity to the sea are proving to be the perfect combination for golf in Gran Canaria. Maspalomas Golf offers a wonderful dune landscape, while Salobre Golf & Resort (exit 53 off GC1) is modern in design, surrounded by a peaceful and quiet environment. Meloneras Golf (exit 50 off GC1) has a cliff-top setting overlooking the sea. Further along the coast, five minutes from Puerto Mogán, Anfi Tauro Golf offers a stunning oasis among palm trees, lakes and volcanic mountains.

comfortable cane chairs that induce a relaxing atmosphere to enjoy great cocktails.

➕ H8 ✉ Hotel Meliá Tamarindos, Calle Las Retamas 3, San Agustín ☎ 928 76 25 66 ◑ Fri–Sat 10.30pm–4am

GARBO'S DINNER SHOW

www.garbos.es
Garbo's offers a show-stopping night among plush surroundings. Singing waiters serve dinner while you sit back and watch the Broadway-style show, currently with a rock music theme. Reservations essential.

➕ J8 ✉ Nordotel SA, Carretera General del Sur km 44, Bahía Feliz ☎ 928 15 70 60 ◑ Show Jul–Apr Wed–Sun 7.30–midnight (Fri from 9.30)

GRAN KARTING CLUB

www.grankarting.com
Claims to be the largest go-kart track in Spain, with three circuits that cater for all ages, even children from five years.

➕ J8 ✉ Carretera General del Sur km 46, Bahía Feliz ☎ 928 15 71 90 ◑ Oct–Apr daily 10–9; May–Sep 11–10

HAPPY BIKING

www.happy-biking.com
Bike excursions for any-one who enjoys riding a bicycle, plus bike hire at a daily rate. The company also arranges hiking tours and buggy safaris.

➕ H9 ✉ IFA Hotel Continental, Avenida de Italia

2, Playa del Inglés ☎ 928 76 68 32 ◑ Mon–Sat 8.30–7

HARLEY'S CAFÉ DANCING

www.harleys-dancing.com
The coolest of the DJ bars that are competing to get noticed in Puerto Rico's commercial centre, complete with shiny Harley Davidson motor-cycles displayed across the bar.

➕ E8 ✉ 2nd floor, CC Puerto Rico, Puerto Rico ◑ Nightly 6pm–3.30am

PACHA

www.pachaplayadeingles.com
Pacha has clubs all over the world but this is among the best. Mainstream dance and pop music pulls in an older crowd, and when things get too hot

inside you can relax on comfy sofas on the terrace, sipping a delicious, cool cocktail.

➕ H9 ✉ Avenida Sargentos Provisionales 10, Edif. Maritin Playa, Playa del Inglés ☎ 928 76 37 11 ◑ Nightly 8pm–4am

PRETTY HORSE CLUB

Enjoy the beautiful valleys and mountains of Gran Canaria on horseback. Horses suitable for beginners or experienced riders go on one- to three-hour treks.

➕ G8 ✉ Carretera de los Palmitos, Finca 4 ☎ 685 01 10 71

SUBMARINE ADVENTURE

Take an exciting journey to the bottom of the sea, aboard a yellow submarine, and discover the fascinating marine life living on the seabed.

➕ E8 ✉ Pantalán Dique Sur, Harbour Puerto Mogan ☎ 928 56 51 08 ◑ Daily tours at 10, 11, 12, 13, 14, 3.30, 4.20 5.10

LAS TIRAJANAS AUDITORIUM

All kinds of artistic performances are held in this contemporary auditorium. The shape of the amphitheatre ensures you get a good view of the stage.

➕ G9 ✉ Plaza de las Convenciones, Urbanización de les Meloneras, Maspalomas ☎ 928 12 80 00

Restaurants

PRICES

Prices are approximate, based on a 3-course meal for one person.

€€€   over €24
€€   €12–€24
€   under €12

ANNO DOMINI (€€€)

The location on the upper floor of the *centro commercial* should not deter you from this sophisticated restaurant, where Chef Jacques Truyol adds a hint of Canarian flavour to his excellent French cuisine.

🔢 H8 ✉ Calle Las Talias, San Agustín ☎ 928 76 29 15 🕐 Dinner; closed Sun and May–Sep

APOLO XI (€€)

A pleasant waterfront spot serving traditional Canarian food, focusing on fresh fish caught the same day.

🔢 F9 ✉ Paseo Maritimo, Arguineguín ☎ 928 73 50 65 🕐 Lunch, dinner

BAR COFRADÍA DE PESCADORES (€€)

This simple restaurant may have plastic tablecloths and paper serviettes, but it also has a far-reaching reputation for its excellent cooking featuring fish straight off the boats in the harbour.

🔢 F9 ✉ Avenida del Muelle s/n, Arguineguín ☎ 928 15 09 63 🕐 Lunch, dinner; closed Mon

BOCCALINO (€€)

www.restauranteboccalino.com

Overlooking Las Burras beach, bright tablecloths, yellow walls and friendly staff make this family-run restaurant an inviting place to eat. Many come especially for the paella and fresh fish.

🔢 H8 ✉ Playa de Las Barras, San Agustín ☎ 928 76 60 18 🕐 Lunch, dinner; closed Sun

LA BODEGUILLA JUANANÁ (€€)

With chunky wooden chairs, large ceramic plates and terracotta pots, this place has a charming and down-to-earth Canarian ambience. Cooking includes local produce from their own deli, prepared in unexpected ways.

FRESH FISH

Fish restaurants here pride themselves on really fresh fish. Even with fish abundant in the waters surrounding the island, demand can often outstrip supply, and good, fresh fish is expensive, even if it is straight from the fishing boats. Tuna, cod, hake, swordfish, mackerel and sardines are available on most menus, but you should sample other local varieties like *cherne* (similar to bass), *sama* (like sea bream) and, a Gran Canarian specialty, *vieja* (like parrotfish).

🔢 E8 ✉ Local 390, Harbour Puerto de Mogan ☎ 928 56 50 44 🕐 Lunch, dinner

LA CANTINA (€€–€€€)

Dark wood panelling and stone flooring, and bottles from the extensive wine list stacked above the bar, set the scene for fine Spanish and Italian cooking. The menu features dishes that specialize in Italian salamis, sausages, ham and Spanish cheese.

🔢 E8 ✉ Apartments El Greco, Calle Doreste y Molina 38, Puerto Rico ☎ 928 56 03 56 🕐 Lunch, dinner

LA CARACOLA: SEEMUSCHEL (€€€)

www.seemuschel.com

A delightful little fish restaurant passionately run by the German owners. The fresh, crisp atmosphere provides an ideal setting for Chef Dieter's creative, perfectly cooked dishes. Reservations are essential.

🔢 E8 ✉ Local X-12 2, Harbour Puerto de Mogán ☎ 928 56 54 86 🕐 Dinner; closed Sun and mid-May to Sep

LA CASA VIEJA (€€–€€€)

On the outskirts of San Fernando, on the road to Fataga, is this rustic, ranch-style restaurant with communal tables that encourage a fun, lively atmosphere. Chargrilled meats are cooked on a vast open grill.

H8 El Lomo, Carretera de Fataga, San Fernando ☎ 928 76 90 10 🍴 Lunch, dinner

CHIPI-CHIPI (€€)

Small, unpretentious café/restaurant with a shaded patio shielded from the busy Avenida Tirajana by attractive glass partitioning. Well-presented food crosses a wide spectrum from salads to steaks and fish dishes.

H9 Avenida Tirajana 19, Edificio Barbados 1, Playa del Inglés ☎ 928 76 50 88 🍴 Lunch, dinner

LAS CUMBRES CANARIAS (€€)

The shepherds' crooks and sheeps' bells that decorate the walls give an indication to the specialty here—roast lamb. This traditional Spanish restaurant is a unique find in a resort full to the brim with international cuisine.

H9 Avenida de Tirajana 9, Playa del Inglés ☎ 928 76 09 41 🍴 Lunch, dinner; closed end Apr–end Jun

EL FARO (€–€€)

Not known for its wonderful cuisine, but the original lighthouse at the end of the harbour wall is a lovely spot for lunch or a coffee while taking in what is probably the best panoramic view of Puerto de Mogán.

E8 Harbour Puerto de Mogán ☎ 928 56 52 85 🍴 Lunch, dinner

LA FORESTA (€€–€€€)

www.riu.com
One of Maspalomas's top hotels opens its doors so non-residents can also enjoy this superb poolside buffet, which will never leave you hungry. When you've had your fill take a walk around the extensive lush gardens.

G9 Hotel Riu Grand Palace Maspalomas Oasis, Playa de Maspalomas ☎ 928 14 14 48 🍴 Lunch

FUSION RESTAURANT AND LOUNGE BAR (€€)

A relative newcomer to Arguineguín, this restaurant and chill-out lounge is fast becoming the most popular place to be seen. Enjoy tasty

---

MOJO SAUCE

Mojo sauce is a standard accompaniment to Canarian cuisine, and dishes containing it are included on many menus. There are many varieties of the sauce, but the most common types are *mojo picón* (spicy red *mojo*) and *mojo verde* (green *mojo*). Complete recipe books are devoted to the subject, and you find *mojo* in jars stacked on shop shelves so you can buy a bottle to take home and try out your own recipes.

South Asian cuisine in sophisticated laid-back surroundings and soak up the sea views.

F9 Calle Alonso Quesada 13, Arguineguín ☎ 928 18 56 62 🍴 Lunch, dinner

GORBEA (€€€)

www.hotelgloriapalace.com
Standing in an elevated position, the views from this ninth-floor hotel restaurant are stunning. Basque cooking with the emphasis on seafood is served in the sunny dining room with large picturesque windows or out on the veranda.

H8 Hotel Gloria Palace, Calle Las Margaritas, San Agustín ☎ 928 12 85 00 🍴 Dinner; closed Sun, May and Jun

LOS GUAYRES (€€€)

www.cordialcanarias.com/los_guayres
Aléxis Álvarez, one of the best-known Canary Island chefs, creates innovative Canarian fusion dishes in a lovely setting. The romantic veranda overlooks a decorative water feature, ideal for a special occasion.

E8 Hotel Cordial Mogán Playa, Avenida de Canarias, Puerto de Mogán ☎ 928 72 41 00 🍴 Dinner; closed Sun and Mon

MAXIMILIAN'S (€€)

Swish waterfront café that promotes total relaxation with large, comfy swivel chairs and plush sofas. It's

mostly pizza, pasta and salad on the menu but the addition of a new restaurant in 2007 has provided a more extensive choice.

➕ G9 ✉ Boulevard El Faro, Maspalomas ☎ 928 14 09 85 🕐 Lunch, dinner

MUNDO (€€)

www.mundorestaurante.com
Black and white checks and a splash of red create a cool, minimalist feel, and the fusion cooking is equally trendy. The set price lunch is popular with the young crowd who dine here.

➕ H9 ✉ Apartmentos Tenesor, Avenida de Tirajana, Playa del Inglés ☎ 928 77 61 41 🕐 Lunch Mon–Fri, dinner Mon–Sat

PATIO CANARIO (€€–€€€)

White pueblo-style building where vines ramble over a shaded patio that is decked with wooden benches and potted plants. Although fresh fish is popular, there are the usual grills as well.

➕ E8 ✉ Local 141, Harbour Puerto de Mogán ☎ 928 56 54 56 🕐 Lunch, dinner

EL PORTALÓN (€€€)

Chef Jose Cruz López brings the flavours of the Basque country to this elegant restaurant inside the Hotel Sol Barbacán. Fern green and white table settings laid with sparkling cutlery and

glassware complement the fine cooking.

➕ H9 ✉ Hotel Sol Barbacán, Avenida Tirajana 27, Playa del Inglés ☎ 928 77 20 30 🕐 Lunch, dinner

QUÉ TAL (€€€)

Striking décor, white leather chairs and contemporary table settings, set the scene for the seven-course tasting menu of international delights to come. Booking is essential.

➕ H9 ✉ Harbour Puerto de Mogán ☎ 928 56 55 34 🕐 Lunch, dinner

RESTAURANTE COFRADIA (€€)

A simple fisherman's cooperative beside the harbour that is not so simple anymore but still producing the best fresh fish in town. Creative chefs cook in the sparkling stainless

VEGETARIANS

Despite the quality and abundant variety of local vegetables available, vegetarians may well feel neglected in Gran Canaria's restaurants. To most of the island's chefs, a meal consisting only of vegetables is a novel concept. Even a so-called vegetable stew is likely to have blood sausage added for supposed extra nutrition, and likewise when you order a salad, it is best to say you don't want tuna.

steel kitchen, which is totally exposed to the stylish dining area.

➕ E8 ✉ Dársena Exterior del Puerto, Puerto de Mogán ☎ 928 56 53 21 🕐 Lunch, dinner

RIAS BAJAS (€€€)

www.riasbajas-playadelingles.com
Below street level is this pristine fish restaurant decorated in cool blue tones. Only the best fish and seafood is used in the dishes mainly influenced by the Galician region of Spain.

➕ H9 ✉ Edificio Playa del Sol, Avenida de Tirajana, Playa del Inglés ☎ 928 76 40 33 🕐 Lunch, dinner

TAGOROR (€–€€)

www.restaurante-tagoror.com
This fascinating cave restaurant burrows into the mountainside high on the *barranco* amid stunning scenery. The menu focuses on true Canarian favourites.

➕ J5 ✉ Montaña las Tierras 21, Barranco de Guayadeque ☎ 928 17 20 13 🕐 Lunch, dinner

TU CASA (€€)

This classy café/ restaurant is housed in an original stone building. The high ceilings and wooden beams remain intact inside, and there is a beachfront terrace.

➕ E8 ✉ Avenida de las Artes 18, Playa de Mogán ☎ 928 56 50 78 🕐 Lunch, dinner

Central Gran Canaria

Take a day trip into the centre of the island and you will be rewarded with the most dramatic scenery from mountain to crater, pine forest to deep ravine. You could visit an ancient cave site of the early inhabitants of Gran Canaria or hike up the stark Roque Nublo or Roque Bentaiga.

GC21

Artenara

1773
Moriscos
GC210

Cruz de Tejeda

GC150

GC210

-15 **Tejeda**

GC60

Cueva Grande

GC150

que aiga

La Culata

GC600

1803

Roque Nublo

GC130

GC60

1951
Pico de las Nieves

1473
tana de arones

Ayacata

Ayacata

La Culata

Risco Blanco

1173
Altos de la Aguililla

GC60

1499
Peñón de la Arena

1035
Montaña las Tierras

San Bartolomé de Tirajana

Tirajana

Santa Lucía

Temisas

alse hira

Cercados de Araña

1535
Morro de la Cruz Grande

GC65

GC60

Cuevas Blancas

GC552

1315
Morro de la Hierba Huerto

La Data

912
Morro Teheral

Fataga

Embalse de Tirajana

GC60

GC65

La Angostura

1036
Montaña Alta

Fataga

1109
Roque Almeida

Fortaleza Grande

Embalse de Gambuesa

Los Vicentes

Tirajana

Arteara

1002
Cerro Puercos

G   **H**   **J**

Andén Verde

TOP 25

Where the cliffs meet the sea—the craggy scenery round Andén Verde

THE BASICS

★ E4
🍴 Cafés and restaurants in San Nicolás de Tolentino and Agaete. Van selling snacks and drinks at the *mirador* (not at all times)
🚌 101 San Nicolás de Tolentino–Gáldar

HIGHLIGHTS

● Mirador del Balcón
● Corniche drive
● Spectacular views

TIP

● Be sure you have plenty of fuel before undertaking this drive as there are no filling stations between San Nicolás de Tolentino and Agaete. Many petrol stations in this area are closed on Sunday afternoons.

A spectacular—if hair-raising—coastal corniche reaches its climax at the Andén Verde or 'Green Platform' just north of San Nicolás de Tolentino. The views from here are awesome.

Mirador del Balcón This is one of the few points where you can actually get the car off the road and truly appreciate the view. Walk down the stone steps to the lower platform and you can look out over the rugged coastline and see the headland at Punta Góngora to your right. To your left are the massive cliffs that gradually decrease in size from the jagged precipices of the Bajones de Ana down to the harbour at Puerto de la Aldea. From here, too, you should be able to see the island of Tenerife to the west across the water. If you can take binoculars, the extra detail will make the views even more spectacular, and if you are lucky you might spot some dolphins basking out at sea.

Driving on Some of the cliffs along this stretch rise to a massive 1,000m (3,280ft), formed by the collapse and subsequent erosion of the north-western part of the original volcano that formed the island some 14 million years ago. The highest point is Roque Faneque at 1,007m (3,293ft). Driving on from the *mirador* the road twists along the cliffs before heading inland around a series of tortuous bends to arrive at the small village of El Risco. From here a dirt track leads down to a pebbled beach. The road then continues back along the coast and on to the town of Agaete.

Whitewashed houses of Artenara (left); the Christ statue (middle); cliffside path (right)

Artenara

Dominated by a huge statue of Christ, Artenara is Gran Canaria's highest town at 1,219m (4,134ft) above sea level. Come here for some of the best views of the central landscape.

Cave dwellings One of the oldest settlements on the island, Artenara's first inhabitants lived in caves hewn from the rock. Many are still lived in today; some are second homes for people from Las Palmas, some let out as holiday cottages, and some are used as refuges for shepherds. The biggest attraction is the fascinating cave chapel, the Santuario de la Virgen de La Cuevita (the Sanctuary of the Virgin of the Cave). Hewn out of the red volcanic rock, it is just 8m (26ft) across. Inside it has a vaulted wooden roof, an altar, a pulpit, choir stand and a confessional. In a niche you can see the carved wooden statue of the Virgin, with the infant Christ in her arms.

Artenara town There are several arts and crafts workshops in the town and it is possible to buy products directly. Items for sale include traditional pottery and handmade Canarian tablecloths. In nearby Lugarejo there is a crafts and pottery centre, all items are made using local materials. Artenara is good place to try local Canarian cuisine. Specialties include grilled pork and rabbit, local cheese and small jacket potatoes served with the spicy sauce, *mojo*. You can also try *ropa vieja*, a chickpea, potato and meat stew; *bienmesabe*, a confection made with ground almonds; and *truchas*, pies filled with sweet potato and fried.

THE BASICS

www.artenara.es
➕ G4
🍴 Cafés and restaurants
🚌 220 from Las Palmas

HIGHLIGHTS

● Cave dwellings
● Cave church
● Fine views
● Local crafts
● Local cuisine

TIP

● Because of its altitude Artenara can get cold in winter and be chilly even on summer evenings—so come prepared.

Fataga

HIGHLIGHTS

● Picturesque houses
● Cobbled alleyways
● Views
● Wine and bodegas
● Apricot festival

TIPS

● You could combine a trip to Fataga with a drive along the spectacular gorge, the Barranco de Fataga.
● Take a camel ride at the Camel Safari Park, at La Barranda on the Maspalomas road.

A picture-postcard village perches on a hillock in a valley surrounded by cliffs, palms and orchards. The well-restored white houses, topped by charming pink-tiled roofs, are especially photogenic.

Picturesque village Only around 20 minutes by car from the southern resorts and a No. 18 bus ride from Maspalomas brings you into another world, revealing just how diverse the island is. The locals describe their homes as *tipico, pequeño y bonito* (traditional, small and pretty) and take great pride in their village, which they are happy to show off to visitors. The tightly packed houses are set around cobbled alleys that are a pleasure to stroll and the views beyond are spectacular. The tiny church, built in 1880 and surrounded by shady trees, is also worth a visit.

Clockwise from far left: Fataga has a pretty hillside setting; traditional plastered house; the steep ridges of the Barranco de Fataga; the red roofs of the village houses form an attractive contrast with the white walls

Authentic souvenirs There are craft and souvenir shops on the main road—selling Canarian products including pottery, shawls and wickerwork—and several bars and cafés. Relax in the square before taking the dramatic drive down the gorge, the Barranco de Fataga, known as the 'Valley of a Thousand Palms'.

Wine and apricots There are several bodegas in the village—this is an important wine-growing region and part of the *denominacíon de origen* Gran Canaria dedicated to producing good quality wine. Check out the Bodega Tabaibilla for some good examples. The village also depends on the hundreds of orange trees that give a wonderful display of colour in October and November. Every year in June the Fiesta del Albaricoque, an apricot festival, is held and the whole village celebrates.

THE BASICS

⊞ H6
🍴 Cafés and restaurants
🚌 18 from Maspalomas

Fortaleza Grande

TOP 25

Modern sculpture at Fortaleza Grande (left); stark scenery surrounds the site (right)

THE BASICS

✚ H6

✉ 4km (2.5 miles) south of Santa Lucía de Tiranjana

🍴 Cafés at Santa Lucía

♿ None

HIGHLIGHTS

● Spectacular scenery
● Pre-Hispanic site of historical interest
● Annual festival in April

TIP

● The Fiesta de los Aborigines on 29 April is marked by ceremonies, music and dancing events.

This fortress-like rock, also known as the Fortaleza de Ansite, commands a dominant position and is surrounded by spectacular scenery. It was the final stronghold of the Guanches in their struggle with the Spanish.

A tragic scene Caves within this rock, a natural volcanic fortification, were inhabited by the Guanche people and also used as burial sites. An abundance of archaeological material has been uncovered. Following their defeat by the Spanish at Roque Bentaiga (▷ opposite) in 1483 the people were urged to surrender by their former king Tenesor Semidan, who had joined the Spanish and become a Christian. Ignoring this command, some of the 1,000 women and 600 men who had retreated to the Fortaleza threw themselves over the cliffs to their death rather than surrender. They were said to have called out to Atis Tirma, their god, as they fell.

Commemoration Each year on 29 April there is a memorial service on the rock remembering the courage of those who died that day in 1484, and a roadside sculpture marks the site of the tragedy. With the final defeat, the fate of the Guanches was sealed; some were sold into slavery; others joined the Spanish, converted to Christianity and received land or tenancies. By 1600 the language and culture of the native people had all but disappeared, although evidence of their existence can be found in sites throughout the island and their spirit is kept alive at annual festivals and events.

Roque Bentaiga

Scenery around the outcrop (left); Roque Bentaiga at sunset (right)

The Guanche people deemed this dramatic rocky outcrop, thrown up by volcanic eruptions over 3 million years ago, a sacred place. Its inaccessibility accounted for its other purpose, a place of refuge.

Former settlement The 1,404m (4,606ft) rock lent itself to protecting the early inhabitants of the island, especially during the Spanish conquest, and its caves were used as shelters. Archaeological digs have also uncovered burial sites, barns and cattle pens. Other remains include rock carvings and paintings. There is evidence of fertility symbols and several rock engravings, and the Libyan-Berber alphabet has been found etched on the walls, although there are doubts about its authenticity. In the eastern side of the base of the *roque* is the *almogarén,* a place of worship for the Guanches, where a big rectangle has been hewn from the rock with a circular dip in the middle. Access to the caves is now restricted, but there is a small information centre by the parking area at the foot of the monolith.

Cuevas del Rey This artifical cave complex, built in pre-conquest times, is located about 2km (1 mile) from Roque Bentaiga along the tortuous road from the Bentaiga/El Espinillo turning. The main cave, the Cueva del Guayre, is one of the largest manmade caves in Gran Canaria, measuring 20m (66ft) long and 11m (36ft) wide. The various rooms inside were used as living areas, granaries and for worship.

THE BASICS

✚ G4
✉ 4km (2.5 miles) south-west of Tejeda
🍴 Cafés and restaurants at Tejeda
❓ Only accessible by car, then half an hour's climb on a track from the parking area

HIGHLIGHTS

● Spectacular views, especially at sunset
● Archaeological remains
● Cave dwellings

TIP

● The roads around this area are particularly difficult, so be prepared to take your time.

★ TOP 25

Roque Nublo

Roque Nublo close up (left); on the hike up (middle); Tejeda lies below (right)

THE BASICS

✚ G5

✉ 2km (1.2 miles) north of Ayacata, off the Ayacata–Cruz de Tejeda road

🍴 Van sells snacks and drinks in car park (not always); roadside bars and restaurants in Ayacata

🚌 18 from Maspalomas to Ayacata, then on foot. Check timetable before setting out

❓ Park your car at La Goleta on the minor road between Ayacata and Cruz de Tejeda

HIGHLIGHTS

● Spectacular views
● The climb
● Volcanic landscape

TIPS

● Start your walk early to avoid crowds in the car park.
● Take something warm to wear at the summit.

This enormous basalt rock known in English as Cloud Rock culminates in a monolith over 64m (210ft high). Although not the highest point on the island it dominates the central region.

Rugged landscape The Roque Nublo soars to a height of 1,803m (3,552ft) above sea level and arose as a result of volcanic activity during the Pleistocene age. The monolith at the summit and a smaller rock, El Fraile, or the Friar, which lies close by to the northeast, have been formed by long-term erosion by water, wind, snow and ice. El Fraile is so named as it is reminiscent of a praying monk in a flowing cassock. Roque Nublo so dominates the landscape it is said that its distinctive silhouette can be seen from as far away as the dunes of Maspalomas. The Spanish writer and philosopher Miguel de Unamuno (1864–1936) was struck by the weathered craggy terrain and described it as 'a storm turned to stone'.

The walk The most direct route to the summit takes just under an hour starting on a well-marked wide path. It is a straightforward climb but not to be underestimated, and you will need to take plenty of water. Once on the ridge you will have fine views of Ayacata (▷ 83). You can decide to circuit around the rock or take a higher path to the summit. From the top there are great views over the town of Agaete and you can see Tenerife on the horizon and Las Palmas to the northeast. Only serious climbers should attempt to scale the rock face.

Canary pines at Tamadaba (left); panoramic view over the pine forest (right)

Tamadaba

The pine forest of Tamadaba is a welcome reminder that Gran Canaria is not all about sea, sun and nightlife. The beauty of this central area is light years away from the coastal resorts.

National park The natural surroundings of the town of Artenara (▷ 75) are becoming a big draw for visitors as the authorities push to promote rural tourism in Gran Canaria. The area designated at a Parque Nacional comprise the Tamadaba Nature Park, a woodland zone with a diverse variety of flora and superb landscapes, and the impressive Tamadaba Pine Grove, the area of greatest ecological value to the island. At 13sq km (5sq miles) in area, and with stunning views, its trails and pathways are a walker's paradise. Viewpoints and paths are well signed and there are maps of the area displayed as well as picnic areas for public use.

Highest peak The pine forest climbs the high slopes of Montaña de Tamadaba, 1,444m (4,736ft) high. This area is a World Biosphere Reserve and contains many other plants other than the Canary pine, including rare flowers and shrubs. The hard wood of the pine is used to make ceilings and balconies. The summit can be reached on a short walk by way of a path that starts from the forest drive; a longer, more strenuous walk starts from Artenara, 8km (5 miles) away. On a clear day it is possible to see Spain's highest mountain, Mount Teide on Tenerife, which is 3,718m (12,195ft) high and over 60km (37 miles) away.

THE BASICS

➕ F3
✉ 8km (5 miles) from Artenara; 57km (35 miles) west of Las Palmas
🍴 Cafés and restaurants at Artenara
🚌 220 from Las Palmas to Artenara

HIGHLIGHTS

● Spectacular views
● Many lovely walking opportunities
● Picnic sites
● Rare flowers and shrubs

CENTRAL GRAN CANARIA

★ TOP 25

More to See

ARTEARA

This village is the location of the island's most important Guanche burial site. At the southern end of the village is a necropolis with hundreds of graves. Informative panels transform the piles of rocks and rubble into some semblance of understanding. You may see camels near here, as the camel safari takes this route.

➕ H7 ✉ 10km (6 miles) north of Playa del Inglés 🚻 Free access 🍴 Cafés and restaurants in Fataga 🚌 18 from Maspalomas

AYACATA

Overshadowed by the massive Roque Nublo (▷ 80), Ayacata is perfectly situated for visitors destined to climb the peak, with souvenir shops, cafés and restaurants to tempt you. There are some wonderful views too, and if you are fortunate enough to visit in February the pretty little church is festooned with almond blossom.

➕ G5 ✉ 42km (26 miles) southwest of Las Palmas; 35km (21 miles) north of Playa del Inglés 🍴 Roadside bars, cafés and restaurants 🚌 18 from Maspalomas

CRUZ DE TEJEDA

The cross of Tejeda marks an important crossroads not far from the central point of the island. Once used by pilgrims, shepherds and traders, today it has become the hub of tourism for the central mountain region. The carved stone cross is set in the square full of stands selling cheap souvenirs and offering donkey rides. Tourists stop here for the good Canarian cuisine served in the local restaurants.

➕ Q4 ✉ 2km (1 mile) from Tejeda; 37km (23 miles) southwest of Las Palmas; 35km (21 miles) north of Playa del Inglés 🍴 Food stands and restaurants

EMBALSE DE SORIA

For something a bit different visit this tranquil reservoir, which is probably one of the best places for fishing on the island. It is popular for swimming and for walkers weary from their trek up the *barranco*.

➕ F6 ✉ 87km (54 miles) southwest of Las Palmas; 35km (21 miles) northwest of Playa del Inglés 🍴 Restaurants in nearby village

The King's Tomb in Arteara's Parque Arqueológico (above); Embalse de Soria (opposite)

Cruz de Tejeda

SAN BARTOLOMÉ DE TIRAJANA

This town is the administrative centre of the municipality that oversees the resorts of the south coast. It's a tranquil place, with mountains to the north and surrounded by orchards and fields, whose claim to fame is the local cherry and rum liqueur, *guidilla*.

✚ H6 ✉ 52km (32 miles) southwest of Las Palmas; 24km (15 miles) north of Playa del Inglés 🍴 Restaurants and cafés 🚌 18 from Maspalomas; 34 from Agüimes

SANTA LUCÍA

Just 3km (2 miles) southwest of San Bartolomé, Santa Lucía is a pretty mountain village solidly devoted to agriculture, and with its own liqueur, *mejunje*, made from lemons, rum and honey. It is also visited for its mock castle museum, the Museo Castillo de la Fortaleza, displaying a hotchpotch of fascinating unrelated artefacts. There is a good rustic restaurant, Hao (▷ 86), which can be overloaded with coach parties.

✚ H6 ✉ 45km (28 miles) southwest of Las Palmas; 31km (20 miles) north of Playa del Inglés 🍴 Restaurants and cafés 🚌 34 from Agüimes

TEJEDA

It's a shame that so many people miss this large village en route to the Cruz de Tejeda, as it is a delight. Fortunately Tejeda and the surrounding area have now recovered from the devastating forest fires of July 2007. Come for the delicious almond biscuits and, if you can, for the almond festival in February.

✚ G4 ✉ 37km (23 miles) southwest of Las Palmas; 78km (48 miles) north of Playa del Inglés 🍴 Bar in village 🚌 305 from Las Palmas; 18 from Maspalomas

TEMISAS

Beautifully set halfway up a mountain this attractive village, with its white-stone houses, is worth a visit. It is the only place on the island to produce olive oil commercially.

✚ J6 ✉ 35km (22 miles) south of Las Palmas; 33km (20 miles) north of Playa del Inglés 🍴 Bar in village 🚌 34 from Agüimes

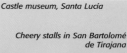

Castle museum, Santa Lucía

Cheery stalls in San Bartolomé de Tirajana

Drive into the Central Highlands

This drive takes you away from the coast, up one *barranco* and back down another, twisting through narrow roads.

DISTANCE: 115km (71.5 miles) **ALLOW:** 5 hours

START

PLAYA DEL INGLÉS
H9

❶ Take the coast road to Arguineguín (▷ 58). At the roundabout behind the cement factory, turn right under the motorway for Cercados de Espinos.

❷ Continue north into the *barranco*. At Cercados de Espinos (12km/7.5 miles), take the slip road through the village. Soon a steep, zigzag climb begins, with wonderful views.

❸ At El Baranquillo Andrés (6km/4 miles), take a left turn signed Mogán and Tejeda. An asphalt road ascends through Z-bends to meet the main road ascending from Mogán.

❹ Turn right here for Tejeda. The road soon runs close to a reservoir— Embalse de la Cueva de las Niñas— where there are good picnic spots. Continue 14km (8.5 miles) northeast through mountainous terrain for Ayacata (▷ 83).

END

PLAYA DEL INGLÉS

❽ After a stiff climb out of the *barranco,* the road passes Mundo Aborigen (▷ 53) and continues to Playa del Inglés.

❼ Return to Ayacata and turn left to San Bartolomé. Follow signs for Fataga. A hairpin descent takes you into the much-admired Barranco de Fataga, passing Fataga village (▷ 76–77) and Arteara (▷ 83).

❻ Continue through pine woods, finally taking a right turn for Las Pechos, arriving at Pico de las Nievas. This part of the route offers fine views, as the ravine walls begin to narrow, of the great Roque Bermejo across the valley to the east.

❺ Turn right towards San Bartolomé de Tirajana (▷ 84). After 200m (220 yards) turn left, climbing to pass Roque Nublo car park.

Restaurants

CUEVA DE LA TEA (€€)

Enjoy some good views from the terrace of this unpretentious restaurant that specializes in roast meat. Try the rabbit (*conejo*) with almonds.
➕ G4 ✉ Calle Hernández Guerra, Tejeda ☎ 928 66 62 27 ⊕ Lunch (until 8pm)

LA ESQUINA (€€)

The terrace at this restaurant is one of the best vantage points in Artenara. The typically Canarian menu boasts classic local dishes such as *potaje de berros* (watercress stew) and the local specialty *tortillas de calabaza* (pumpkin pancakes).
➕ G4 ✉ Calle Párroco Domingo Báez, Artenara ☎ 928 66 63 81 ⊕ Mon–Sat lunch

LA HACIENDA DEL MOLINO (€€€)

www.lahaciendadelmolino.com
Delightful rustic-style restaurant/hotel lovingly restored to re-create the original Canarian building. The cuisine, too, is true to its Canarian roots. You can see the *gofio,* the stoneground flour made from roasted cereals, being prepared at the restored mill.
➕ H6 ✉ Calle Los Naranjos 2, Tunte, San Bartolomé de Tirajana ☎ 928 12 73 44 ⊕ Lunch, dinner

HAO (€€)

It does get busy here with tourists visiting the nearby museum of Canarian life but it serves good Canarian food at heavy wooden tables. Grilled meat is the specialty, and you can also try the local liqueur, *mejunje,* here.
➕ H6 ✉ Calle Tomás Arroyo Cardosa, Santa Lucia de Tirajana ☎ 928 79 80 07 ⊕ Daily 9–7

TAKE A PICNIC

Restaurants are few and far between in the mountainous centre of the island and as an alternative there are a number of roadside picnic areas set up by the environment agency. All have wooden tables and benches; some also have barbeques, toilets, drinking water and play areas. The most popular include Pinar de Tamadaba (near Artenara); Montaña de Santiago (between Ayacata and the Chira reservoir); Llanos de la Paz (on the road from Roque Nublo to Cruz de Tejeda) and Cueva de las Niñas (southwest of Ayacata on the GC605 by the reservoir).

MIRADOR DE SANTA LUCÍA (€€)

Dine with a view at this attractive restaurant in the pretty mountain village of Santa Lucía. The menu offers both international and Canarian cuisine.
➕ H6 ✉ Calle Maesto José Enriquez Hernández 5, Santa Lucía de Tirajana ☎ 928 79 80 05 ⊕ Daily 9am–1am

RESTAURANTE LA ALBARICOQUE (€)

Right in the centre of Fataga, this charming stone house has a lovely outdoor terrace and gorgeous mountain views. The friendly owners serve good, wholesome Canarian cuisine and a few dishes with a more international flavour. They also have two apartments if you fancy a stay.
➕ H6 ✉ Calle Nestor Alamo 4, Fataga ☎ 928 79 86 56 ⊕ Wed–Mon lunch (until 5pm)

RESTAURANT CENTENNIAL (€€–€€€)

www.hotelruralelrefugio.com
This is a popular port of call for people visiting Cruz de Tejeda. Housed in the rural hotel El Refugio, the wood-panelled restaurant has plenty of exposed stone and terracotta tiles on the floor. If you are ravenous after walking in the mountains you will be rewarded with delicious Canarian fare.
➕ G4 ✉ Cruz de Tejeda ☎ 928 66 65 13 ⊕ Lunch

The North

The lush, fertile hills and valleys in the north of Gran Canaria provide an ideal terrain for walking. The area is cloudier than the sun-baked south coast, but offers spectacular coastline, rugged ravines, dramatic archaeological sites and pretty market towns—all without the crowds.

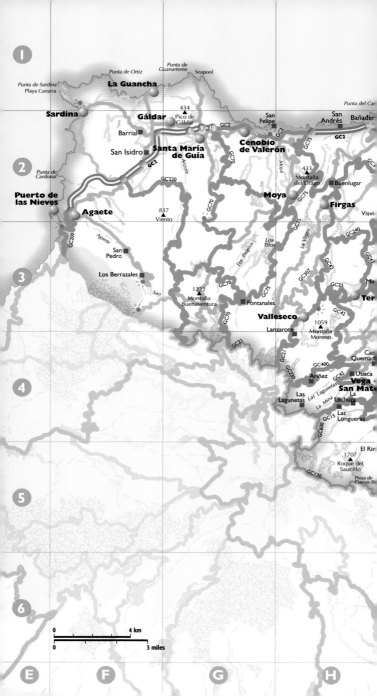

Caldera de Bandama

TOP
25

HIGHLIGHTS

● Spectacular views of volcanic scenery
● Good walking
● Pico de Bandama *mirador*

TIPS

● Wear good, sturdy shoes for the walk down into the crater and take some water.
● The Pico de Bandama mirador is a 30-minute walk from the bus stop.
● Be aware that the road to the *pico* is closed every night 10pm–8am.

For the best view down into the *caldera* (crater), drive up the steep spiralling road to the *mirador* on the adjacent peak, Pico de Bandama (754m/1,833ft). From here the huge, stunning crater spreads out before you.

Perfectly formed The Bandama crater is 1km (0.6 miles) across and 200m (656ft) deep, in the classic perfect bowl shape. It was named after a Dutchman, Daniel van Damm, who planted vines here in the 16th century. You can take a walk down into the fertile valley floor but bear in mind that though the walk down may be easy, the only way out is to make the steep ascent back up. There is a clearly marked path leaving from the small hamlet on the road above. Allow at least an hour and half for the hike there and back. The

The dramatic bowl of the Bandama crater (left and below) makes a unique setting for the lush golf course at its edge (bottom; ▷ 104)

path starts well but can be slippery farther down. If you don't want to go all the way there is a *mirador* with great views about halfway down. At the bottom there is another clearly defined path around the crater floor.

What's in the crater After transcending the slopes of dark grey ash the landscape is transformed, with olive trees, cactus, borage and broom adding a touch of greenery. At the centre of the crater is an abandoned wine press dating back to the 18th century. The lone farmhouse has been occupied by a single farmer who keeps chickens and goats and tends a mix of fruit trees. From here the path climbs back out of the crater. On the way up keep an eye open for a group of Guanche cave dwellings dramatically set into the crater wall.

THE BASICS

✚ K4

✉ 2km (1 mile) south of Tafira Alta; 10km (6 miles) south of Las Palmas, reached via GC110 from Las Palmas

🍴 Bar in village (opening times vary); restaurant at Hotel Golf Bandama

🚌 311 from Las Palmas

Cenobio de Valerón

TOP 25

A honeycomb of caves lies sheltered under a great basalt arch

THE BASICS

www.cenobiodevaleron.com

⊞ G2

✉ 3km (2 miles) east of Santa Maria de Guía; 21km (13 miles) south of Las Palmas. It can be reached from the town or the GC2 Las Palmas–Agaete road

☎ 618 60 78 96

🕐 Apr–Sep Tue–Sun 10–6; Oct–Mar Tue–Sun 10–5

🚌 103, 105 from Las Palmas

♿ None

🎟 Inexpensive

HIGHLIGHTS

● Cave complex
● Views
● Guided tour

The Cenobio de Valerón is the most impressive and the largest pre-Hispanic fortified granary in Gran Canaria. Its precarious position made it virtually impregnable to attack.

Natural food larder The Cenobio is located in the Cuesta de Silva and can be reached from Santa María de Guía or from the Las Palmas–Agaete road. Volcanic rock, known as toba or tosca, was soft enough to hollow out using wooden and stone implements into some 300 chambers, which were used for storage and linked by a network of steps and passages. This indicates the importance of agriculture to the early inhabitants of the island. As with most caves the temperature and humidity remained constant, ensuring the grain kept its quality. Many of the grain 'silos' have grooves, indicating they had lids or doors, mostly made of wood or stone or occasionally skins or vegetable fibre. By putting an ashy mortar around the lid the contents could be kept airtight.

Rejected story The word *cenobio* translates as 'convent' and early commentators believed that this place was a Guanche nunnery, where daughters of nobility and *harimaguadas* (vestal virgins) were watched over by priests and priestesses prior to marriage. Although such places did exist, the position of this complex points to the fact it was a communal grain store and the previous theory has been rejected. The site was closed for a while for safety reasons, but has now been improved, and you can visit on your own or join a guided tour.

Church of Santa Maria (left); shelves laden with local cheeses (right)

Santa Maria de Guía

Founded in 1483, Guía, as it is more commonly known, is one of the oldest towns in Gran Canaria. You need to seek out its old quarter to find some of the island's most attractive architecture.

Guía buildings Beyond the modern buildings on the outskirts of Guía is a charming yet elegant centre with cobbled streets fanning out from a leafy main square. The town was classified as a National Historical and Artistic Monument in 1982 and among its best-preserved buildings is the church of Santa Maria. Its neoclassical façade is flanked by two towers and was designed by sculptor Luján Pérez, who was born in Guía in 1756. Take a look at the house of the Quintana family at No. 3 Plaza Mayor, a fine example of Canarian architecture, with its typical wooden balcony and family coat of arms displayed above the door.

Cheese town You really can't visit this town without tasting its cheese. The specialty cheese *flor de Guía* or *queso de flor* (flower cheese) is one of the island's most popular food products. It is produced by curdling fresh milk from cows and sheep or goats with thistle—a species of artichoke—flowers. It is cured on beds of reeds in dry caves, giving it its unusual smell and flavour. It can be bought at the shop of Santiago Gil Romero (▷ 104) where the cheese is matured on bamboo mats. Once piled to the rafters with cheese and a conglomeration of press cuttings and other items, the shop has now been slightly tidied up but it is still a delight to visit.

THE BASICS

www.santamariadeguia.es

✚ G2

✉ 23km (15 miles) west of Las Palmas; 76km (47 miles) northwest of Playa del Inglés

🍴 Cafés in town

🚌 103, 105 from Las Palmas

HIGHLIGHTS

● Colonial architecture
● Church of Santa Maria
● *Queso de flor*

THE NORTH ★ TOP 25

Jardín Botánico Canario

- Plaza de Viera y Clavijo
- Islands garden
- Cacti and succulents
- Canary pinewood
- Laurel forest
- Dragon trees
- Fountain of the wise

TIP

- It can be confusing that there are two entrances to the garden. The best entrance is the upper one, with more parking and the nearest bus stop.

These gardens, the largest in the whole of Spain, are devoted to the conservation of the Canarian flora. The archipelago of the Canary Islands can boast some 2,000 species, 500 of which are endemic, many of which are on display here.

Setting up The full title of the gardens is the Jardín Botánico Canario Viera y Clavijo named after the illustrious 18th-century naturalist and historian Don Jose de Viera y Clavijo, whose white stone bust watches over the landscape from the lookout at the top of the garden. The gardens were actually founded in 1952 by the Swedish botanist Eric Sventenius who did much of initial planning, classifying and planting. Research, conservation and education are foremost in the development of the gardens.

Clockwise from left: Native succulents; manicured lawns in the bottom of the barranco; *hardy shrubs; red hot pokers* (Kniphofia) *are native to Africa*

A tour of the gardens Most visitors arrive at the top entrance, which gives a good view across the gardens and down the 150m-high (500ft) *barranco*. The 27ha (67 acres) of ground are divided into a string of different gardens. You can explore at random but it is a more logical approach to follow the gardens through from the lower entrance and work back to the top. The Jardín de las Islas gives an insight into the native plants of the islands. Further highlights include the prickly cacti—which include endangered species grown with the intention of replanting them in their natural habitat—and the succulent plants, Canary pines, laurel forest, waterfalls and fountains. On your way back to the viewpoint you can pass through the 'dragon-tree walk'. Pick up a plan of the gardens to guide you round. For more information about the plants you can visit the small exhibition centre.

THE BASICS

www.jardincanario.org

➕ J3

✉ Tafira Alta, 7km (4 miles) south of Las Palmas, GC110 road (top entrance)

☎ 928 21 95 80

🕐 Daily 9–6

🍴 Jardín Canario restaurant (▷ 106)

🚌 301, 302, 303, 305. Ask the driver to drop you at the gardens (top entrance)

♿ Limited—lower entrance only, off GC310

🖐 Free

Teror

HIGHLIGHTS

● Basilica
● Casa de los Patronos de la Virgen
● Plaza del Pino
● Plaza Teresa de Bolívar
● Canarian architecture

TIP

● Visit on market day, when stalls are set up behind the basilica.

The showpiece town of Gran Canaria is resplendent with whitewashed houses and cobbled streets. Teror is also a pilgrimage centre for inhabitants of the island, as its basilica houses the Virgin of the Pine, the patron saint of the island.

Superb architecture The attractive houses sport typical wooden Canarian balconies, some of which have ornate carving. The basilica is in the large Plaza del Pino; it was begun in 1760 though there have been changes and restoration programmes over the subsequent centuries. The present church has a gabled roof and three apses with 14 Roman arches supported by columns and pilasters. The altar of Our Lady of the Pine is a centre of pilgrimage for the people of the island. On this site, as legend has it, the Virgin appeared in a pine tree

Delicately carved balconies grace the traditional houses of Teror (left); basilica of Our Lady of the Pine (below); carved stone benches and Gothic fountain in Plaza Teresa de Bolívar (bottom)

to the first bishop of Gran Canaria, Juan Frías, in 1492. A religious festival is held on 8 September, culminating in celebratory singing and dancing.

The high life The charming Casa de los Patronos de la Virgen is a museum dedicated to the Canarian gentry and their lifestyle. A perfect example of a traditional Canarian town house, it has been owned by the Manrique de Lara family since the 17th century, and displays family heirlooms and furniture in room settings.

Other gems Don't miss the delightful garden square Plaza Teresa de Bolívar, named after the first wife of the revolutionary Simon de Bolívar. Teresa grew up in Teror, the daughter of a noble family. Sadly she died of yellow fever less than a year after her marriage in 1801.

THE BASICS

www.teror.es

✚ H3

✉ 21km (13 miles) south-west of Las Palmas

🍴 Cafés around Plaza del Pino

🚌 216 from Las Palmas

Casa de los Patronos de la Virgen

✉ Plaza del Pino

☎ 928 63 02 39

🕐 Mon–Fri 11–6, Sun 10–2

♿ Ground floor only

💲 Inexpensive

More to See

AGAETE

www.aytoagaete.es

This maritime town, in the north-west of the island, benefits from low rainfall and some 2,400 hours of sunshine a year. It's an attractive place with typical Canarian houses and a pleasant central square with its grandiose 19th-century church. There are several arts and crafts shops and a good selection of restaurants, with local grilled fish a specialty.

🚹 F2 ⊠ 37km (23 miles) west of Las Palmas 🍴 Restaurants and cafés 🚌 103 from Las Palmas

ARUCAS

www.arucasturismo.com

If you thought the town's parish church was a cathedral it would not be surprising. The building, dating from 1909 and built entirely of local Arucas stone, is most impressive with richly engraved pillars and fine stained glass windows. Arucas is famous for its rum distillery and the Museo del Ron (Rum Museum: Era de San Pedro 2, tel 928 62 49 00; Mon–Fri 10–2;

free admission). A visit to the premises consists of a tour and a taste of the end product. If you are interested in gardens, take a look at the Jardín de la Marquesa (Mon–Sat 9–1, 2–6) on the edge of town. The house was built in 1880 and though you can't go inside, the delightful Romantic gardens, complete with Japanese pavilion, are worth a visit. There are some 2,500 species here, many of them endemic to the island.

🚹 J2 ⊠ 18km (11 miles) west of Las Palmas 🍴 Restaurants and cafés 🚌 205, 206, 210 from Las Palmas

LA ATALAYA

Once a village consisting purely of cave houses, visiting today you will find some free standing houses and original cave dwellings with added extensions. The inhabitants of the village are famous for their unglazed pottery. All is made in the original style, without a wheel, and hand-shaped using the volcanic clay. A pottery centre in the town preserves the techniques and traditions of the

Ornate church of San Juan Bautista, Arucas

Waterfall down Paseo de Gran Canaria, Firgas

art founded by Francisco Rodriguez Santana, better known as Panchito, who died in 1986 and learned all his skills from his mother.

➕ J4 ✉ 5km (3 miles) west of Santa Brígida; 12km (8 miles) south of Las Palmas 🚌 105, 311 from Las Palmas

FIRGAS

Most of the small town of Firgas falls inside the Doramas Rural Park, an area of special natural interest, and the drive to the town takes you through some picturesque country-side. Take a look at the old town centre and check out the Paseo de Gran Canaria, a pedestrian walkway where a natural gradient has been used to incorporate a striking 27m (90ft) waterfall with brightly tiled benches to one side. There is also a 16th-century *gofio* mill. The town pro-duces mineral water for distribution throughout the island.

➕ H2 ✉ 10km (6 miles) southwest of Arucas; 25km (15.5 miles) west of Las Palmas 🚌 201, 202 from Las Palmas; 211 from Arucas

GÁLDAR

www.galdar.es

Gáldar was the capital of the Guanche kingdom of Guanartematos and the surrounding area is full of important archaeological sites. Now a centre of the banana industry, the town is worth a visit for its interesting architecture and an excellent covered market (Thu 8–2). It is possible to buy some local items in the town including Canarian knives, pottery and woodwork, with some fine examples of traditional musical instruments, furniture and farming implements. Don't forget to take home some of the cheese made with flowers.

➕ G2 ✉ 10km (6 miles) southwest of Arucas; 27km (17miles) west of Las Palmas 🍴 Restaurants and cafés 🚌 103, 105 from Las Palmas

MOYA

www.villademoya.com

Spectacularly perched on the edge of a deep ravine, the town of Moya has a rich cultural heritage. The present church of Our Lady of Candelaria is

Moya stands at the top of the Barranco del Pinar

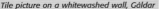

Tile picture on a whitewashed wall, Gáldar

positioned high on the cliffs over-looking the *barranco*. It was built in 1957 on the same site where former churches have collapsed into the ravine. In front of the church is the house where the poet Tomás Morales was born in 1884, which now houses a museum devoted to his life and works (Plaza de Tomas Morales, tel 928 62 02 17; Mon–Fri 9–8, Sat 10–8, Sun 10–2; admission free).
✚ H2 ✉ 25km (15 miles) west of Las Palmas 🍴 Restaurants and cafés 🚌 116, 117 from Las Palmas; 123 from Arucas

PUERTO DE LAS NIEVES

This coastal village has a lovely harbour, a marina and a couple of beaches. There may be no sand but the water is clean and you can dive and surf. Everywhere there are connections with the sea—even the church is adorned with model boats and this is the place to sample the freshest of fish.
✚ F2 ✉ 39km (24 miles) west of Las Palmas 🍴 Fish restaurants 🚌 103 from Las Palmas

SARDINA

Sardina beach is particularly popular with locals for its smooth sands and good sea conditions making it ideal for watersports. To avoid the crowds try visiting mid week. Located right in the northwest corner of the island it is sheltered and something of a suntrap. When you've had enough of the beach try one of the seafront restaurants that specialize in seafood and fresh fish.
✚ F2 ✉ 33km (20 miles) west of Las Palmas 🍴 Cafés and fish restaurants 🚌 103, 105 from Las Palmas to Gáldar, then taxi to Sardina

TELDE

www.telde.es
Telde is Gran Canaria's second city with a population of over 8,000. Seek out the old quarter of San Francisco with its narrow streets and pretty houses with typical wooden balconies and pitched tiled roofs. Churches include the 18th-century San Francisco and San Juan Bautista, attractively set in a pleasant square

Old quarter of Telde

Aerial view of Puerto de las Nieves

in the north of the town. Take a look inside at the life-size figure of Christ. You can also visit the former home of the architect of the harbour at Las Palmas, León y Castillo. Souvenirs to buy in the town include baskets, knives, pottery and handicrafts.

➕ K4 ✉ 21km (13 miles) south of Las Palmas 🍴 Cafés and restaurants 🚌 12, 80 from Las Palmas; 36, 90 from Maspalomas

VALLESECO

This predominantly agricultural village sits in the most beautiful of regions, often overlooked by visitors. The area is criss-crossed with excellent pathways and ancient trails, providing first-class hiking opportunities in woods and ravines. Close by is the most recent volcano on Gran Canaria, Montañón Negro, which has been declared a national monument because of its geological significance. It is possible to buy some traditional craft products in and around the village. Produce is another option depending on the season—chestnuts, walnuts, apples, oranges and plums

can all be bought. Try, too, the local *milflores* honey or the honey wine.

➕ H3 ✉ 28km (17 miles) southwest of Las Palmas 🍴 Cafés and restaurants in the area 🚌 220 from Las Palmas

VEGA DE SAN MATEO

www.vegasanmateo.com

In a dramatically placed location with a backdrop of mountains, this pleasant agricultural town is worth a visit. 'Vega' means 'fertile' and the carefully tended terraces on the hillside reflect the local economy and you can sample the produce at the traditional market held on Sunday mornings, which also sells local craft items. To continue the agricultural theme visit La Cantonera historical centre on Avenida Tinámar, one of the island's most important ethnographic museums. It is located in a 17th-century farmhouse and contains over 12,000 items of furniture, farm implements, handicrafts and much more.

➕ H4 ✉ 21km (13 miles) southwest of Las Palmas 🍴 Cafés and restaurants 🚌 303 from Las Palmas

Basketware for sale in Vega de San Mateo

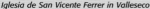
Iglesia de San Vicente Ferrer in Valleseco

Around the Island

This long tour offers a glimpse of fishing villages, mega-resorts, volcanic scenery, fertile valleys and a dramatic coastal corniche.

DISTANCE: 176km (109 miles) **ALLOW:** 6 hours, plus possible detours

START

NORTH OF LAS PALMAS
➕ K2

END

SOUTH OF LAS PALMAS
➕ K2

❶ Start on the motorway (GC2) running west along the north coast from Las Palmas. Keep on this road as it bypasses Gáldar towards Agaete. When the motorway runs out, turn right to visit Puerto de las Nieves (▷ 100).

❷ Take the road to Agaete (▷ 98), then turn right, following signs to San Nicolas de Tolentino. This stretch yields magnificent views, but make sure you have plenty of fuel.

❸ The road turns inland to isolated El Risco, where a valley bed planted with gardens leads down to a beach. The view grows ever more dramatic as you drive along the Andén Verde corniche.

❹ As the road begins its slow descent, pull into the parking area at Mirador Balcón. Follow the GC200 inland to San Nicolas de Tolentino (▷ 61), with the Roque Nublo (▷ 80) visible in the distance.

❽ Continue on the coast road towards Arguineguín (▷ 58). From here rejoin the GC2 motorway to skirt the south coast resorts and follow the somewhat unappealing coastline back to Las Palmas.

❼ From here take the GC500 coast road, which hugs the cliff, passing a string of newer resorts. You will then come round the bend and Puerto Rico (▷ 60) is laid out up the steep hillsides ahead.

❻ Continue straight through the centre of Mogán (▷ 60) along a fertile valley to the delightful resort of Puerto de Mogán (▷ 56–57).

❺ At San Nicolas turn right before a windmill and follow signs to Mogán. The road twists and turns inland, eventually climbing into the foothills.

DRIVE

THE NORTH

Shopping

LA ATALAYA CENTRO LOCERO
www.centrolocerolaatalaya.org
Since times long passed the village of La Atalaya has been an outstanding centre of pottery production. At this centre, not only are there items for sale, you can also learn about the process.
J4 Camino de la Picota 11, La Atalaya ☎ 928 28 82 70

CASA DEL VINO DE GRAN CANARIA
In this lovely old building wine lovers can sample every variety of wine the island has to offer before deciding what to buy.
J4 Calle Calvo Sotelo 26, Santa Brígida ☎ 928 64 42 72

DESTILERÍAS AREHUCAS
www.arehucas.es
At the Arucas rum factory you are encouraged to taste before you buy. Light and dark rums, some aged for 12 years, along with rum-based liqueurs flavoured with coffee, banana, orange, honey and almonds.
J2 Lugar Era de San Pedro 2, Arucas ☎ 928 62 49 00

SANTIAGO GIL ROMERO
One of the best places to buy cheese is this fascinating shop owned by the Romero family. The family share their love of cheese with their customers, offering samples to try insisting you wash it down with a glass of wine.
G2 Calle Marqués de Muni 34, Santa María de Guía ☎ 928 88 18 75

Entertainment and Activities

EL CORTIJO CLUB DE CAMPO
www.elcortijo.es
An 18-hole course opened in 2000, 6km (4 miles) south of Las Palmas. There is also a pitch and putt course that is illuminated at night.
L4 On GC1 km 6, near Telde ☎ 928 71 11 11

PICADERO REAL CLUB LAS PALMAS
A riding centre that offers lessons and organized treks through dramatic rural landscape. Beginners and experienced riders are welcome. There are a total of 50 stables and five paddocks, and some wonderful countryside in which to take a hack.

YO HO HO AND A BOTTLE OF RUM
Sugarcane was a huge crop in the area around Arucas, and it was from this resource the famous rum was born. The factory in Arucas is distinguished in the town by its high, narrow chimney. Opened in 1884, it quickly became the base of the town's economy. The factory's cellars hold about 6,000 oak casks, which guarantee the highest quality products.

K4 Lugar de Bandama s/n, Santa Brígida ☎ 928 35 10 50

REAL CLUB DE GOLF DE LAS PALMAS
www.realclubdegolfdelas palmas.com
The oldest golf club in Spain, located on the edge of the Bandama crater and just 15 minutes' drive from Las Palmas. Undulating 18-hole course with narrow fairways. The site also has a hotel and restaurant, plus mini golf, tennis and horse riding (▷ far left).
J4 Carretera de Bandama s/n, Santa Brígida ☎ 928 35 01 04

Restaurants

PRICES

Prices are approximate, based on a 3-course meal for one person.
€€€   over €24
€€   €12–€24
€   under €12

ASADERO LAS BRASAS (€)

An informal barn-like restaurant popular with locals for its chickens roasted in charcoal grills. Good, home cooking at reasonable prices.

🔲 H2 ✉ Avenida de la Cruz 36, Firgas ☎ 928 62 52 50 🕐 Lunch, dinner

BALCÓN DE LA ZAMORA (€€)

www.larutadelbuenyantar.com/zamora.html
Zamora is always busy with the passing coach parties, who flock here for the beautiful, panoramic views from the mountains down to the coast. The food is traditional Canarian; the kid stew is a more unusual favourite.

🔲 H3 ✉ Carretera General Valleseco 13, near Teror ☎ 928 61 80 42 🕐 Lunch, dinner; closed Fri

BODEGÓN VANDAMA (€€–€€€)

www.larutadelbuenyantar.com/vandama.html
Grilled meats accompanied by fine wines are the focus of this country retreat. A grape press stands right in the middle of the bright and airy dining area, which has a typical rural Canarian atmosphere.

🔲 K4 ✉ Monte Lentiscal 116, Carretera de Bandama ☎ 928 35 27 54 🕐 Closed Sun dinner, Mon and Tue

CÁPITA (€€)

As pretty as a picture, with its gingham table-cloths and hanging ivy, this welcoming, family-run seafood restaurant is considered by many locals as the best of its kind in the area.

🔲 F2 ✉ Calle Nuestra Señora de las Nieves 37, Puerto de las Nieves ☎ 928 55 41 42 🕐 Lunch, dinner; closed Tue–Fri dinner and Mon

CASA PEPE (€€)

In the idyllic Agaete Valley, Casa Pepe is one of the most frequented establishments in the area. A warm greeting

CHEESE

In Gran Canaria cheese *(queso)* is often found on the menu as a starter rather than an after a meal course. The most common varieties are *queso tierno* (a soft goat's cheese), *queso curado* (mature sheep's or goat's cheese, such as Majorero from Fuerteventura) and *queso de flor*, Gran Canaria's most renowned cheese produced in the highlands of Guía and curdled with thistle flowers.

is extended to all guests, which creates an informal atmosphere. Recommended dishes include the grilled prawns.

🔲 F2 ✉ Calle Alcalde Armas Galván 5, Agaete ☎ 928 89 82 27 🕐 Lunch, dinner; closed Wed

CASA ROMÁNTICA (€€)

International and Spanish dishes are served at this delightful restaurant using the freshest produce—it's come direct from the restaurant gardens. It is often busy with coach groups touring the Valle of Agaete.

🔲 F2 ✉ Carretera Los Berrazales, km 3.5, Agaete ☎ 928 89 80 84 🕐 Noon–6pm

EL CASTILLETE (€€)

Select and cook your own meat at the barbecue or on a hot stone at your table, in rustic surroundings. Other specialties include Segovia-style suckling pig and roast leg of lamb. Very popular, so reserve ahead at weekends.

🔲 J4 ✉ Calle El Raso 3, La Atalaya ☎ 928 35 24 43 🕐 Lunch, dinner; closed Sun and Mon dinner

LA CUEVA (€€)

Peach tones and wooden chairs help create a soothing mood at this small cave restaurant. The cooking style is Canarian and fresh fish features strongly on the menu.

THE NORTH

RESTAURANTS

There is a terrace outside if you prefer to eat under natural light.
➕ G2 ✉ Avenida Alcalde Antonio Rosas 80, Playa de Sardina, Gáldar ☎ 928 88 02 36 🕐 Lunch, dinner; closed Tue in winter

FANEQUE (€€€)
Off the beaten track, this upscale restaurant in the Hotel Puerto de las Nieves offers the finest products of the islands, prepared with great care, as well as a select list of wines.
➕ F2 ✉ Avenida Alcalde José de Armas, Puerto de las Nieves ☎ 928 88 62 56 🕐 Lunch, dinner; closed Mon

FRAGATA (€€€)
www.restaurantelafragata.net
Select your own fish, lobster or crab at this smart seafront restaurant with wide-open views. The interior resembles the inside of a frigate.
➕ F2 ✉ Avenida Alcalde Antonio Rosas, Playa de Sardina, Gáldar ☎ 928 88 32 96 🕐 Lunch, dinner; closed Sun dinner and Wed

LAS GRUTAS DE ARTILES (€€€)
www.lasgrutasdeartiles.com
The dining areas in this fascinating cave restaurant are connected by tunnels. Outside there are lovely grounds with tennis courts and a swimming pool. It has earned itself a reputation for delicious, Canarian classics.

➕ J4 ✉ Las Meleguinas, Santa Brígida ☎ 928 64 05 75 🕐 Lunch, dinner

JARDÍN CANARIO (€€€)
Looking out onto the Barranco Guiniguada above the beautiful botanical gardens, this family-run spot is ideal for a peaceful lunch or dinner. The food includes excellent grilled meats and the homemade desserts are delicious.
➕ J3 ✉ Carretera del Centro km 7, Tafira Alta ☎ 928 43 09 24 🕐 Lunch, dinner

EL MESÓN DE LA MONTANA (€€–€€€)
The wide variety of both traditional Spanish and some more unusual fare on the menu is popular with tourists, but really the main reason for coming here is the spectacular views.

SANCOCHO
Sancocho is a favourite traditional meal on the island. It is the sort of meal served to the whole family for Sunday lunch, causing much smacking of lips and kissing of fingers—but it may be an acquired taste. It is a dish of salt *cherne*, a fish like bass (the saltier the better), served with boiled potatoes and *gofio*, either in dumpling form or as a thickening agent in the gravy.

➕ J2 ✉ Montana de Arucas, Arucas ☎ 928 60 08 44 🕐 Lunch, dinner

MIGUELÍN (€€)
A mishmash of objects hang on the walls of this simple fish restaurant, which prides itself on a good value and friendly service. Each dish is freshly prepared and cooked to order.
➕ F2 ✉ Carretera de Sardina del Norte km 5, Gáldar ☎ 928 88 00 15 🕐 Lunch, dinner; closed Mon

TERRAZA EL ANCLA (€€)
On the promenade, this fish restaurant resembles a *chiringuito* (beach huts that were once common in all Spanish fishing ports). Ask for the fresh catch of the day, which usually comes grilled, with toasted garlic and herbs— simple but delicious.
➕ F2 ✉ Avenida Antonio Rosas, Playa de Sardina ☎ 928 55 14 96 🕐 Lunch, dinner

LA VEGUETILLA (€€€)
www.larutadelbuenyantar. com/veguetilla.html
In a villa surrounded by lush gardens, La Veguetilla is tastefully decorated— simple yet elegant. You can enjoy the beautifully cooked Spanish and Canarian cuisine out on the terrace if you like.
➕ H4 ✉ Carretera del Centro 129, Vega de San Mateo ☎ 928 66 07 64 🕐 Lunch, dinner

If you have not booked through a tour operator, the best place to look is on the internet, where special deals are often available. From luxury hotels to hostels, you should be able to find something to suit your needs.

Introduction

Most visitors to the island come on a package holiday, which includes accommodation. For those looking for somewhere to stay on arrival, the airport or local tourist information offices should be able to help but it is better to book in advance.

Hotels Around the Island

All establishments are graded by the Canarian government from one to five stars, and three-star hotels and above will have a private bathroom. Although the weather is good year round, there are still high and low seasons (▷ 114) and price and availability will vary accordingly.

Self-catering

This is particularly popular with families and cheaper than staying at a hotel. Apartments are graded from one to three keys and most comprise bedroom(s), bathroom, living area, small kitchen and balcony or terrace. Linen, towels and maid service are included. Apartments are often only available for a full week's let at a time.

Staying in the Country

With the upsurge in rural tourism on the island, a holiday in the country is becoming increasingly popular. A perfect base for hikers or nature lovers, rural hotels vary from the basic to luxurious. Some will have swimming pools, bike hire and horse riding and some include the opportunity to have an evening meal. *Casas rurales* are self-catering accommodation that can be village houses, cave homes or farmhouses converted to cottages for rent.

CHOOSING YOUR LOCATION

It is possible to find a hotel for just a few days if you wish to make the journey from the south coast up to Las Palmas. If you decide to stay on the south coast, choose your resort carefully, as they range from the brash and lively to quiet and sedate. Grand luxury hotels can be found along the beach at Maspalomas and Meloneras.

From top: Apartments, Puerto Rico; Hotel Escuela, Santa Brígida; Patalavaca; Hotel Princesa Guayarmina

Budget Hotels

LOS CASCAJOS

This is a great place to stay if you want to take a break during a drive around the island. For a reasonable price you get a simple but clean room and friendly service. 20 rooms.

➕ D5 ✉ Calle Los Cascajos 9, San Nicolás de Tolentino ☎ 928 89 11 65

HOSTAL ALCARAVANERAS

www.canaryhostel.com

In a good location nearer the smaller beach of Playa de Alcaravaneras and near to the main shopping street of Avenida Mesa y López, this Las Palmas hostel is basic but clean and friendly and offers free internet access and Wi-Fi in all the rooms. 20 rooms.

➕ b2 ✉ Calle Luis Antúnez 22, Las Palmas ☎ 928 24 89 14 🚌 1, 12, 13, 17

HOTEL MADRID

Maybe not the most comfortable or modern hotel, but a place that oozes character—you can even stay in the room where Franco slept (room 3). The fun-loving brothers who run this hotel are gradually upgrading the 17 rooms.

➕ c5 ✉ Plaza de Cairasco 4, Las Palmas ☎ 928 36 06 64 🚌 2, 3, 30, 90

HOTEL PRINCESA GUAYARMINA

Located in the stunning Valle de Agaete you can pick up some good deals at this charming little spa hotel. Perfectly placed for walks in the countryside, you can also relax on the pool terrace and admire the view. 33 rooms.

➕ F3 ✉ Los Berrazales, Valle de Agaete ☎ 928 89 80 09

HOTEL REGINA MAR

Surrounded by gardens and palm trees, this hotel is just 300m (328 yards) from the beach and close to all the shopping and nightlife

action. The one-bedroom apartments sleep up to three people. There is a restaurant and poolside bar. 133 rooms.

➕ H9 ✉ Avenida de Estados Unidos 38, Playa del Inglés ☎ 928 76 76 16

LIBERTY APARTMENTS

If you want a cheap stay in the centre of the action these apartments are a good deal. Although a little way from the beach they are near shops, restaurants and nightlife. Ask for a room with a view of the pool. 92 rooms.

➕ H9 ✉ Avenida de Tirajana 32, Playa del Inglés ☎ 928 76 74 54

LA LUNA

www.ecoturismograncanaria.com

A great opportunity to stay in a traditional village house at a very reasonable price. The handful of rooms are charmingly decorated and each has its own bathroom. Friendly owners. 3 rooms.

➕ F2 ✉ Calle Guayarmina 42, Agaete ☎ 928 39 01 69

VEROL

In a really great location just a minute from Playa de las Canteras, this unpretentious hotel is good value and pleasantly fitted out. 25 rooms.

➕ a1 ✉ Calle Sagasta 25, Las Palmas ☎ 928 26 21 04 🚌 1, 12, 13, 41

Mid-Range Hotels

ANFI DEL MAR

www.anfi.com

Made up of four different 'clubs' each with a separate identity but all sharing the vast array of facilities for all the family. Swimming pools, tropical gardens, a marina and white sand beach—it has it all. 869 apartments.

🚌 F9   ✉ Barranco de la Berga, Arguineguín   ☎ 928 15 29 90

BLUEBAY BEACH CLUB

www.bluebayresorts.com

Situated above the sea in the quiet resort of Bahía Feliz, this beach club aparthotel is attractively decked out with modern furnishings and boasts a fine pool. There are few restaurants in the immediate vicinity but the hotel has its own à la carte option. 158 apartments.

🚌 J8   ✉ Paseo Pablo Picasso, Bahía Feliz (near San Agustín)   ☎ 928 15 72 19

CASA DE LOS CAMELLOS

Get away from it all at this lovely rural hotel in the charming town of Agüimes, renovated from a 300-year-old stone barn. 12 rooms.

🚌 K6   ✉ Calle El Progreso 12, Agüimes   ☎ 928 78 50 03

GLORIA PALACE

www.gloriapalaceth.com

A large, well-established hotel in the quiet resort of San Agustín. It has two garden swimming pools and a pool on the top floor of the hotel. A thalassotherapy (sea-water therapy) centre offers many treatments.

🚌 H8   ✉ Calle Las Margaritas s/n, San Agustín   ☎ 928 12 85 00

HACIENDA DE ANZO

www.haciendadeanzo.com

A delightful rural hotel in Canarian-colonial style and set in lovely gardens. Great base for hiking and horse riding but you can also just relax by the pool. 6 rooms.

🚌 G2   ✉ Vega de Anzo, Gáldar   ☎ 928 55 16 55

HOTEL CORTIJO SAN IGNACIO GOLF

www.cortijosanignaciogolf.com

This delightful hotel retains its 18th-century

MOVING AROUND THE ISLAND

If you are staying in the south you can always take a couple of days' break in Las Palmas or vice versa. In fact the excellent bus service will enable you to travel cheaply between resorts anywhere around the island. The buses, run by Global Salcai Utinsa (☎ 928 25 26 30; www.globalsu.net), are reliable but always check bus numbers and times in advance.

detail and is set in lovely gardens with a gorgeous pool. The rooms are beautifully decorated and exude charm. The 18-hole golf course is an added bonus. 18 rooms.

🚌 K4   ✉ Autoposta del Sur GC km 1, Telde   ☎ 928 71 24 27

HOTEL GOLF DE BANDAMA

The adjoining golf club is the oldest in Spain and boasts a challenging and beautiful course. The hotel rooms all have a balcony or terrace over looking the course and pool; some overlook the Bandama crater. Also tennis and horse riding. 34 rooms.

🚌 J4   ✉ Carretera Bandama s/n, Santa Brígida   ☎ 928 35 15 38

HOTEL IGRAMAR

www.igramar.com

It's great to be staying in a city yet only be a minute from the beach. Modern, stylish and clean, this hotel also offers access for visitors with disabilities. 61 rooms.

🚌 a2   ✉ Calle Colombia 12, Las Palmas   ☎ 928 47 29 60   🚍 45, 47

HOTEL NEPTUNO

www.neptunograncanaria.com

Not an inspiring building but refurbishment has improved the interior and created a smart, clean hotel in the centre of Playa. Close to all the action with the Yumbo

centre nearby. Good size pool and 171 rooms.
➕ H9 ✉ Avenida Alféceres Provisionales 29, Playa del Inglés ☎ 928 77 74 92

HOTEL PARQUE
www.hparque.com
Nice situation overlooking the park and close to the shops of Triana and the old town, Vegueta. Its proximity to the bus station makes it a good base for visiting the island. Comfortable modern rooms plus top-floor restaurant and sun terrace. Good value. 102 rooms.
➕ c4 ✉ Muelle de Las Palmas 2, Las Palmas ☎ 928 36 80 00 🚌 1, 11, 41

HOTEL PUERTO DE MOGÁN
www.hotelpuertodemogan.com
Formerly the Club de Mar, this small hotel is perfectly located between the marina and the beach. The apartments have a rooftop sun terrace and access to the hotel facilities. 56 rooms and 90 apartments.
➕ E8 ✉ Playa de Mogán, Puerto de Mogán ☎ 928 56 50 66

HOTEL PUERTO DE LAS NIEVES
www.hotelpuertodelasnieves.es
Renowned for its superb hydrotherapy centre, this smart hotel provides a range of water treatments. The hotel has an excellent restaurant, Faneque, specializing in locally caught fish. 30 rooms.

➕ F2 ✉ Avda Alcalde José de Armas, Puerto de la Nieves ☎ 928 88 62 56

HOTEL RURAL MAIPEZ
www.maipez.com
Just 10 minutes from Las Palmas, this delightful rural hotel has spectacular views of the Guiniguada *barranco*. The bedrooms in the restored 200-year-old finca are attractively decorated and retain original features. There's a public restaurant, lovely gardens and three tennis courts. 10 rooms.
➕ J3 ✉ Carretera de La Calzada 104, La Calzada ☎ 928 28 72 72

HOTEL TRYP IBERIA
www.solmelia.com
Panoramic views of the sea are a major attraction at this large,

comfortable hotel next to the Triana commercial district. Beauty centre, swimming pool and gym. 297 rooms.
➕ c4 ✉ Calle Alcalde José Ramírez Bethencourt 8, Las Palmas ☎ 928 36 11 33 🚌 12, 13

IFA BEACH
www.ifahotels.com
Mainly the domain of visitors from Germany and Scandinavia on all-inclusive packages, this hotel is well placed for the beach and has bright rooms, most with sea and pool views. Good buffet breakfast. 200 rooms.
➕ H8 ✉ Los Jazmines 25, San Agustín ☎ 928 77 40 00

EL REFUGIO
www.hotelruralelrefugio.com
Charming rustic hotel with all modern comforts. Cruz de Tejeda gets busy in the day but is peaceful at night. Come for a walking holiday in the mountains and you will be rewarded at the end of the day with this perfect refuge with 10 rooms.
➕ G4 ✉ Cruz de Tejeda ☎ 928 66 65 13

EL VEOR
A beautifully renovated 19th-century country house 20 minutes' walk from Teror. Relax around the pool or use the hotel as a base to visit the lovely surrounding countryside. 3 rooms.
➕ H3 ✉ Los Corrales 48, Teror ☎ 928 39 01 69

WHERE TO STAY MID-RANGE HOTELS

Luxury Hotels

PRICES

Expect to pay more than €120 per night for a double room in a luxury hotel.

H10 PLAYA MELONERAS PALACE

www.h10hotels.com
Set above the quiet Meloneras beach, in lovely landscaped gardens. Inside the traditional Canarian-style structure is contemporary elegance with a choice of restaurants and two bars. Two swimming pools and a health suite round off the facilities. 373 rooms.
🞧 G9 🖂 Calle Mar Caspio 5, Playa Meloneras, Maspalomas
☎ 928 12 82 82

HACIENDA DEL BUEN SUCESO

www.haciendabuensuceso.com
Set in an authentic hacienda-style house at the heart of a banana plantation. With its characterful rooms, this is an ideal spot to be pampered and relax away from the crowds. 18 rooms.
🞧 J2 🖂 Carretera de Arucas a Bañaderos km 1, Arucas
☎ 928 62 29 45

HOTEL CORDIAL MOGÁN PLAYA

www.cordialcanarias.com
This stunning hotel is designed in traditional colonial style, with a dramatic mountain backdrop and lush gardens. Facilities include the reputable Los Guayres restaurant, and swimming pools with an artificial beach. 399 rooms.
🞧 E8 🖂 Avenida de los Marrero, Playa de Mogán
☎ 928 72 41 00

HOTEL REINA ISABEL

www.bullhotels.com
In an unrivalled position on Playa de las Canteras, the Reina Isabel is almost a Las Palmas institution, maintaining a very stylish atmosphere. A rooftop swimming pool and terrace provide privacy and lovely views. 224 rooms.
🞧 a1 🖂 Calle Alfredo L Jones 40, Las Palmas ☎ 928 26 01 00 🖵 1, 2, 3, 12, 13, 41

HOTEL SANTA CATALINA

www.hotelsantacatalina.com
An exquisite English

Colonial-style building that has attracted royalty since the hotel opened in 1890. Dark wood verandas with wicker chairs overlook the tranquil grounds distancing you from the city bustle. 202 rooms.
🞧 b3 🖂 Calle León y Castillo 227, Parque Doramas, Las Palmas ☎ 928 24 30 40 🖵 12, 13

LOPESAN VILLA DEL CONDE

www.lopesanhotels.com
On the seafront at Meloneras, this Canarian-style village has luxurious villa-type rooms, with hanging wooden balconies, set around a lovely pool area and colourful gardens. The dining facilities are excellent. 561 rooms and suites.
🞧 G9 🖂 Mar Mediterráneo 7, Playa de las Meloneras
☎ 928 56 32 00

RIU GRAND PALACE MASPALOMAS OASIS

www.riu.com
This aptly named hotel is one of the most luxurious on the south coast, with direct access to the sand dunes at Maspalomas. Peacocks strut around the extensive grounds, which are simply beautiful and there is every conceivable facility you would expect from a 5-star hotel. 332 rooms.
🞧 G9 🖂 Plaza de las Palmeras 2, Playa de Maspalomas ☎ 928 14 14 48

GOLF IN LUXURY

If golf is your passion then spoil yourself at the Salobre Golf Club Resort & Spa (🖂 Urbanizacion Salobre Golf, Maspalomas ☎ 928 94 30 00; www.starwoodhotels.com). The boutique hotel is set in landscaped grounds next to the Salobre golf course. After a round, relax at one of the seven outdoor pools, or take the free shuttle bus to the beach. At the end of the day, enjoy excellent cusine at one of the three restaurants, while you savour the peace and quiet.

Use this section to prepare for your trip and familiarize yourself with getting around the island—moving around the central regions will probably require your own transport. The Essential Facts will contribute to making your stay a success.

Planning Ahead

When to Go

Gran Canaria is mild year-round; temperatures rarely drop below 15°C (59°F) and the south has over 300 days of sunshine a year. There are two peak seasons: July and August, when Spanish families are on holiday, and January to March. The quietest months are May and June.

TIME

L The Canaries are in the same time zone as the UK (GMT), which is one hour behind most of Europe.

AVERAGE DAILY MAXIMUM TEMPERATURES

JAN	FEB	MAR	APR	MAY	JUN	JUL	AUG	SEP	OCT	NOV	DEC
19°C	19°C	19°C	20°C	21°C	21°C	23°C	24°C	24°C	25°C	25°C	19°C
66°F	66°F	66°F	68°F	70°F	70°F	73°F	75°F	75°F	77°F	77°F	66°F

Spring (April to May) can produce sunshine and showers in April but generally there is no significant change.

Summer (June to August) temperatures in the south often exceed 30°C (80°F).

Autumn (September to October) shows no real change from summer other than a small drop in temperatures.

Winter (November to March) rain falls mostly in the north, and there is occasional snow in the central mountains.

WHAT'S ON

January *Festival of the Three Kings* (6 Jan): gifts for the children.

February *Almond Blossom Festival*: song, dance and almond sweets in Tejeda and Valsequillo.

Carnival season: street bands, parties and parades. The best ones are in Las Palmas and Maspalomas.

March/April *Semana Santa* (Holy Week, last week before Easter) is celebrated everywhere; processions with sacred icons.

April *Fiesta de los Aborígenes* (29 Apr): commemorates the defeat of the aboriginal people at Fortaleza Grande.

May/June *Feast of Corpus Christi*: the streets are decorated with flowers and sand.

June *San Juan* (week around 24 Jun): anniversary of the foundation of Las Palmas, celebrated with concerts, dance, sports events and bonfires on the beach.

July *Fiesta del Carmen* (16 Jul): celebrated by all fishing villages.

Feast day of Santiago (25 Jul): Gáldar and San Bartolomé celebrate with Canarian wrestling, picnics and traditional dancing.

August *Bajada de la Rama* (4 Aug): in Agaete, from an ancient aboriginal rite of praying for rain. Modern Canarians enjoy the chance to get wet and party.

September *Feast of La Virgen del Pino* (8 Sep): pilgrims come from all over the island to Teror.

Fiesta del Charco (10 Sep): everybody gets wet in San Nicolás de Tolentino.

October *Fiestas de Nuestra Señora del Rosario* (5 Oct): celebrated in Agüimes, with Canarian stick-fighting and wrestling.

December *Fiesta de los Labradores* (20 Dec): in Santa Lucía people celebrate by dressing in peasant costumes and carrying old-fashioned farm tools.

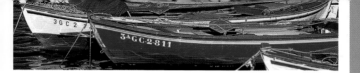

Gran Canaria Online

www.canarias.es
The Canary Islands' official website, with a wealth of visual and practical information about getting to the islands, places to stay, attractions, maps, weather and what's on.

www.grancanaria.com
Gran Canaria's official tourism website includes practical information on the island's sights, accommodation, restaurants, entertainment, events, transport and lots more.

www.spain-grancanaria.com
Information on planning and booking your holiday, plus the most interesting places to visit, and all those essential travel tips you shouldn't leave home without.

www.promocionlaspalmas.com
The chief tourist site for Las Palmas has interesting sections on monuments, tourist attractions and history, and links to other useful sites.

www.maspalomas.com
Official site of the municipality of Villas de San Bartolomé de Tirajana, which incorporates the resorts of Maspalomas, Playa del Inglés and San Agustín; it has useful material that you might not find on other sites, such as street directories.

www.ecoturismocanarias.com
From the Canarian Association for Rural Tourism, this site helps plan a more back-to-nature type holiday and has suggestions for rural accommodation.

www.puertorico-tonight.com
www.maspalomas-tonight.com
Two sites, each packed with good up-to-date information on the resorts' nightlife as well as shopping, restaurants and other leisure attractions.

PRIME TRAVEL SITE

www.spain.info
The main Spanish Tourist Board website carries a wealth of information about the whole country and a section on the Canary Islands—available in several languages.

INTERNET ACCESS

Most of the main towns and resorts have internet cafés (*cibers*) or bars where you can get online, but you may struggle to find somewhere in more rural areas or small towns. Generally it costs around €3–€5 per hour to log on.

Cyber Las Palmas
✉ Calle Tomas Morales 56
☎ 928 43 26 86
🕐 Mon–Fri 10.30am–11.30pm, Sat, Sun 4.30–11.30

Lena's IT-Café
www.lenasitcafe.com
✉ Centro Comercial San Agustín
☎ 928 76 60 63
🕐 Daily 1–11

Getting There

ENTRY REQUIREMENTS

For the latest passport and visa information, look up the British embassy website at www.fco.gov.uk or the United States embassy at www.usembassy.gov or contact the relevant consulate (▷ 121).

TRAVEL INSURANCE

Take out your insurance as soon as you book your trip to ensure you are covered for delays. Most policies cover cancellation, medical expenses, accident compensation, personal liability and loss of personal belongings (including money). Your policy should cover the cost of getting you home in case of medical emergency. An annual travel policy may be the best value if you intend to make several trips in a year, but long trips abroad may not be covered. If you have private medical coverage, check your policy, as you may be covered while you are away.

AIRPORTS

Most visitors arrive on the numerous charter flights direct from Western Europe into Aeropuerto de Gando. Visitors coming from North America may have to fly via Madrid. The flight from London takes approximately four hours and from Madrid approximately two hours.

FROM GANDO AIRPORT

Gando airport (☎ 902 40 47 04; www.aena.es) is about 18km (11 miles) south of Las Palmas and 33km (20 miles) north of Maspalomas. There is a frequent, reliable and inexpensive bus service to Las Palmas and the south (☎ 902 38 11 10 or 928 25 26 30; www.globalsu.net). Bus 60 leaves from outside the terminal to Las Palmas every 45 minutes from 6.45am to 7.45pm; bus 05 operates less frequently throughout the night from 7pm–7am. The journey takes around 35 minutes to the central bus station at Parque San Telmo (cost €2.10), where there are connections to local buses as well as buses to other parts of the island. You can stay aboard to Santa Catalina bus terminal (another 10 minutes; cost €2.70). Bus 66 leaves for Maspalomas Faro every hour from 7am to 10pm. The journey takes around an hour; cost €3.70. From Playa del Inglés there are connections to other south coast resorts, including Puerto Rico and Puerto Mogán.

The quickest and most expensive way to get to Las Palmas or anywhere else on the island is by taxi from outside the terminal building. The

cost to Las Palmas would be around €26 and to Playa del Inglés about €32—there is usually a supplement of €1.65 for airport runs.

ARRIVING BY SEA

The ferry company Trasmediterránea (☎ 902 45 46 45; www.trasmediterranea.com) has services from Cádiz on the Spanish mainland, which arrive at Puerto de la Luz ferry terminal, 13km (2 miles) from Las Palmas. The journey from Cádiz takes around 38 hours. Fred Olsen (☎ 902 10 01 07; www.fredolsen.es) and Naviera Armas (☎ 902 45 65 00; www.naviera-armas.com) also provide similar services.
The journey from Puerto de las Nieves to Las Palmas takes around 40 minutes by road.

FROM OTHER ISLANDS

Most of the Canary Islands have an airport and it is very easy to connect between each one. The main operators are Binter Canarias (☎ 902 39 13 92; www.bintercanarias.com and Islas Airways (☎ 902 47 74 78; www.islasairways.com). Flight times are around 30 minutes, depending on which island you are travelling from, and flights are frequent—from Tenerife there is one almost every hour. Interconnecting flights are well used by islanders so they do get booked up early.

CUSTOMS

Although the Canaries are part of Spain, for customs purposes they do not count as part of the EU. The maximum limits for bringing in or taking out goods are: 1 litre of spirits, 2 litres of still wine, 200 cigarettes, 250ml of eau de toilette, 60ml of perfume and up to €145 worth of other goods. The import or export of wildlife souvenirs sourced from rare or endangered species may be either illegal or require a special permit. Check your home country's regulations before purchasing.

CAR RENTAL

Several of the major car rental companies have offices at the airport, as well as in Las Palmas and the major resorts. To contact a reputable firm where the car can be picked up from the airport call:
Avis ☎ 928 57 95 78; www.avis.com
Europcar ☎ 928 57 42 44; www.europcar.com
Hertz ☎ 928 57 95 77; www.hertz.com
Cicar ☎ 928 57 93 78; www.cicar.com

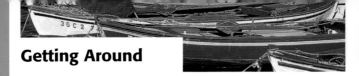

Getting Around

NEED TO KNOW GETTING AROUND

BUSES

www.globalsu.net
Everything you could possibly want to know about the public bus service Global, which serves the complete island. How to buy the best tickets for your needs, timetables, prices, routes, maps–but unfortunately not in English.

TAXI FIRMS

Useful contact details:
● Cooperativa de Taxistas de San Agustín ☎ 928 76 67 67; www.taxisdemaspalomas.com
● Socomtaxi
☎ 928 15 47 77
● Radio Taxi Las Palmas
☎ 928 46 18 18

ORGANIZED EXCURSIONS

As a large proportion of visitors come to Gran Canaria with a package deal, tour operators offer numerous excursions, from bus tours to jeep safaris, which can be booked through the holiday reps. This can be an expensive way of seeing the island but you can relax and let somebody else do all the planning. Local companies sell excursions but beware of something for nothing–it could be combined with a hard-sell timeshare–and only use reputable companies.

Gran Canaria is a comparatively small island and it is possible to drive around the island in one day. Most of the roads are good and well maintained, although in many places the tight, twisting bends can be a challenge. There is a very efficient network of buses that service the entire island and Las Palmas has its own local service. Taxis are plentiful and reasonably cheap.

ISLAND-WIDE BUSES

Global (☎ 928 25 26 30 or 902 38 11 10; www.globalsu.net) operates a comprehensive and economic network of routes to resorts in the south and to many towns and villages in the north and centre, with reasonably frequent departures during the day and some at night. The main hub is at the Parque San Telmo bus station (☎ 928 44 65 00) in Las Palmas, but there are several other terminals at major towns and resorts. Timetables and maps are available from the bus station and in the larger tourist offices, and are posted online and at bus stops. You can pay on the bus, but there are various discount cards available; a *tarjeta insular* is good value if you intend to move around a bit. Available from larger bus stations, it gives you €15 worth of travel at a 20 per cent discount, and is also valid on city buses. Simply tell the driver where you travelling to and insert the card in the machine at the front of the bus so the fare can be deducted.

URBAN BUSES

In Las Palmas, the yellow Guaguas Municipales (☎ 928 07 77 78 or 928 30 58 00; www.guaguas.com) provide a cheap and efficient service. The three most useful routes (Nos. 1, 2, 3) connect the old town to the port. City bus maps and timetables are available from the information office at San Telmo bus station. Some smaller towns such as Telde and Arucas have their own buses. Tickets can be purchased on board and cost a flat rate of €1.20. The *bono-guagua* (€6.50), available from newsagents/bus terminals, gives 10 journeys for the price of six.

The Las Palmas open-top tourist bus is a great way to see the city. Tickets are valid for the whole day and you can get on and off at any stop. The two-hour circuit begins at Parque Santa Catalina and has a commentary in English; tickets are sold on board.

TAXIS

Taxis are usually identified by a green light on the top, which is illuminated when it is free for hire. Most taxis are metered at a rate fixed by the municipal authorities. Some longer journeys outside the municipal boundaries have a fixed rate, so it is advisable to agree a fare in advance. It is acceptable to hail a taxi on the street, but taxi ranks are plentiful, and at busy times it is better to reserve in advance.

DRIVING

If you want to explore away from the coast you will need to rent a car. Local companies compete for your custom so it's worth shopping around for the best deal. To rent a car you must be over 21 and will be asked for your passport, driving licence and credit card. Speed limits are 120kph (75mph) on motorways, 90kph (56mph) on main roads and 40kph (25mph) in built-up areas, unless otherwise stated. The only fast roads on the island are the GC1 motorway from Las Palmas to Puerto Rico and the GC2 from Las Palmas to Agaete. The narrow, twisting mountain roads are often slow so you need to plan plenty of time for your journey.

WALKING

Walking in the mountains is a popular activity on Gran Canaria, particularly with the younger generation. Older folk remember a time when there were few roads on the island and walking was the only method of transport. Caminos Reales, literally 'royal ways' are a network of paths once guaranteed by royal authority. They now form the basis of many of the island's walking tracks.

VISITORS WITH A DISABILITY

Things are slowly improving in Gran Canaria. Las Palmas city buses have some vehicles adapted for wheelchairs, with low floors and extra space, and Global buses operate adapted buses on most routes at least once a day. Most museums can be accessed but lifts are limited, and they offer little for sight- or hearing-impaired visitors. Many restaurants now have wheelchair ramps, and most accommodation provides ample facilities; rural and budget hotels may be less accessible. For details of wheelchair-friendly hotels and attractions contact COCEMFE (☎ 928 71 74 70; www.cocemfelaspalmas.org). ONCE (☎ 915 77 37 56; www.once.es/new/home) is a national body for the visually impaired.

BREAKDOWN ASSISTANCE

The Royal Automobile Club of Gran Canaria (✉ Luis Doreste Silva 3, Las Palmas ☎ 928 23 07 88; www.race.es) offers advice on breakdown and repair services. Repairs are usually dealt with promptly. If you have a rental car, follow the instructions given in your rental documentation and phone the local rental office.

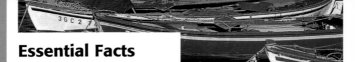

Essential Facts

ELECTRICITY

● The power supply is 220 volts (older buildings 110 volts).

● Sockets take two-pin plugs of round-pin continental style. Visitors from the UK require an adaptor and US visitors a voltage transformer.

MONEY

The euro is the official currency of Spain. Bank notes come in denominations of €5, €10, €20, €50, €100, €200 and €500, and coins in 1, 2, 5, 10, 20 and 50 cents and €1 and €2. Credit cards are widely accepted. ATMs are very common and a good way to withdraw money.

5 euros

10 euros

50 euros

100 euros

MEDICAL TREATMENT AND MEDICINES

● EU citizens are entitled to receive free or reduced medical treatment in the Canaries with the relevant documentation (EHIC card for Britons), although travel insurance is advised.

● For medical emergencies call 112 or go to the *urgencias* department at one of the large hospitals in Las Palmas: Hospital Dr Negrin ☒ Calle Barranco de la Ballena ☎ 928 45 00 00 or University Hospital Insular ☒ Avenida Maritima del Sur ☎ 928 44 40 00.

● There are medical and dental clinics in most towns, some with 24-hour service; your hotel or the local tourist information office will help you find an English-speaking clinic. Dental services have to be paid for by all visitors but is usually covered by private medical insurance.

● Prescription and non-prescription drugs and medicines are available from *farmacias* (pharmacies), distinguished by a large green cross. Outside normal hours, a notice on the door should give the address of the nearest duty pharmacist (see www.farmaciascanarias.com).

● Tap water is generally safe to drink but has a salt content. It is best to drink mineral water, which is widely available and cheap.

● The sun is quite potent, particularly in the south. Use a high-factor sunscreen and avoid the hottest part of the day (noon–3pm).

NATIONAL HOLIDAYS

● 1 Jan: New Year's Day
● 6 Jan: Epiphany
● 19 Mar: St. Joseph's Day
● Mar/Apr: Maundy Thu, Good Fri, Easter Mon
● 1 May: Labour Day
● 30 May: Canary Islands' Day
● May/Jun: Corpus Christi
● 15 Aug: Assumption of the Virgin
● 8 Sep: Birthday of the Virgin Mary
● 12 Oct: Spanish National Day
● 1 Nov: All Saint's Day
● 6 Dec: Constitution Day
● 8 Dec: Feast of the Immaculate Conception
● 25 Dec: Christmas Day

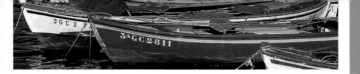

OPENING HOURS

● Shops: generally Mon–Sat 9/9.30–1.30/2, 4.30/5–8. Larger shops don't close for siesta and in busy resorts some are open on Sunday.
● Museums: hours vary, but generally 10–1, 4–8. Many close one day a week.
● Pharmacies: 9–1/2, 4–7.30; many close Saturday afternoon.
● Banks: 9–1/2 but they may stay open longer in winter; closed Sunday.
● Post offices: 9–2 but larger branches stay open much later.

TOURIST OFFICES

● Las Palmas: Patronato de Turismo Gran Canaria (Local Tourist Authority) ✉ León y Castillo 17 ☎ 928 21 96 00; www.grancanaria. com 🕒 Mon–Fri 9–2.
There are also information offices kiosks in Parque San Telmo, Parque Santa Catalina, Avenida Mesa y López, Pueblo Canario, and on the promenade behind Playa las Canteras.
● South Coast: Centro Insular de Turismo Centro ✉ Avenida España (Centro Comercial Yumbo), Playa del Inglés ☎ 928 77 15 50 🕒 Mon–Fri 9–9, Sat 9–1.
Oficina de Información Turística ✉ Centro Comercial El Portón, Local 11, San Agustín ☎ 928 76 92 62; www.maspalomas.com 🕒 Mon–Fri 9–2.
Oficina de Información Turística ✉ Avenida de Mogán, Puerto Rico ☎ 928 15 88 04; www. mogan.es 🕒 Mon–Fri 9–2.
● Most other towns and larger villages have a tourist office, though most close at weekends.

TELEPHONES

● Public telephones are plentiful, with instructions in several languages. Most take coins, credit cards or phonecards, which are sold in post offices, kiosks and shops.
● The cheap rate for international calls is from 10pm to 8am and all day Sunday.
● The code for Gran Canaria is 928, and all numbers prefixed with 900 are toll-free.

EMERGENCY NUMBERS

● Police 112 or local police 928 44 64 00 (Las Palmas); 928 72 34 29 (Maspalomas); 928 56 90 00 (Mogán)
● Fire 112 or 80 (Las Palmas)
● Ambulance 112 or 061
● Coast Guard 062

CONSULATES IN LAS PALMAS

● France: ✉ Nestor de la Torre ☎ 12 928 29 23 71
● Germany: ✉ Albareda 3 ☎ 928 49 18 80
● Netherlands: ✉ Calle León y Castillo 42–5 ☎ 928 36 22 51
● UK: ✉ Luis Morote 6 ☎ 928 26 25 08

SENSIBLE PRECAUTIONS

● Violence against tourists is rare. Theft from cars is the most common form of crime, particularly in Las Palmas.
● At the airport keep your passport, money and other valuables in an inside pocket/ money-belt, and don't leave hand luggage unattended.
● Do not leave anything of value on the beach, by the pool, or in your car.
● When not in use, lock valuables in hotel safe deposit boxes.
● In Las Palmas late at night, avoid the port and Parque Santa Catalina.

Language

Spanish is spoken in the Canary Islands. People working in the tourist industry generally know some English, but if you venture off the beaten track, it's helpful to know some basic Spanish. Pronunciation guide: *b* almost like *v*; *c* before *e* or *i* sounds like *th* otherwise like *k*; *d* can be like English *d* or softer *th*; *g* before *e* or *i* is a guttural *h*, otherwise *g*; *h* always silent; *j* guttural *h*; *ll* like *lli* in million; *ñ* like *ni* in onion; *qu* like *k*; *v* like *b*; *z* like *th*.

COURTESIES

good morning	*buenos dias*
good afternoon/evening	*buenas tardes*
good night	*buenas noches*
hello (informal)	*hola*
goodbye (informal)	*hasta luego/hasta pronto*
hello (answering phone)	*¿Diga?*
goodbye	*adios*
please	*por favor*
thank you	*gracias*
you're welcome	*de nada*
how are you? (formal)	*¿Como está?*
how are you? (informal)	*¿Que tal?*
I'm fine	*estoy bien*
I'm sorry	*lo siento*
excuse me (in a bar)	*oiga*
excuse me (in a crowd)	*perdón*

DAYS

Monday	*lunes*
Tuesday	*martes*
Wednsday	*miércoles*
Thursday	*jueves*
Friday	*viernes*
Saturday	*sábado*
Sunday	*domingo*
today	*hoy*
yesterday	*ayer*
tomorrow	*mañana*

NUMBERS

1	*uno*
2	*dos*
3	*tres*
4	*cuatro*
5	*cinco*
6	*seis*
7	*siete*
8	*ocho*
9	*nueve*
10	*diez*
11	*once*
12	*doce*
13	*trece*
14	*catorce*
15	*quince*
16	*dieciséis*
17	*diecisiete*
18	*dieciocho*
19	*diecinueve*
20	*veinte*

USEFUL WORDS

I don't know	*No lo sé*
I don't think so	*Creo que no*
I think so	*Creo que sí*
It doesn't matter	*No importa*
Where?	*¿Dónde?*
When?	*¿Cuándo?*
Why?	*¿Por qué?*
What?	*¿Que?*
Who?	*¿Quién?*
How?	*¿Cómo?*
How much/many?	*¿Cuánto/cuántos?*
Is/are there?	*¿Hay?*
ticket	*entrada*

BASIC VOCABULARY

yes/no	*sí/no*
I don't understand	*no entiendo*
I don't speak Spanish	*no hablo español*
left/right	*izquierda/derecha*
entrance/exit	*entrada/salida*
open/closed	*abierto/cerrado*
good/bad	*bueno/mal*
big/small	*grande/pequeño*
with/without	*con/sin*
more/less	*más/menos*
hot/cold	*caliente/frío*
early/late	*temprano/tarde*
here/there	*aquí/allí*
today/tomorrow	*hoy/mañana*
yesterday	*ayer*
how much is it?	*¿cuanto es?*
where is the…?	*¿dónde está…?*
do you have…?	*¿tiene…?*
I'd like…	*me gustaría*
my name is…	*me llamo…*

FOOD

apple	*manzana*
banana	*plátano*
beans	*habas*
chicken	*pollo*
clams	*almejas*
duck	*pato*
fish	*pescado*
fruit	*fruta*
lamb	*cordero*
lettuce	*lechuga*
lobster	*langosta*
meat	*carne*
melon	*melón*
orange	*naranja*
pork	*cerdo*
seafood	*marsicos*
shrimps	*gambas*
squid	*calamare*
tomato	*tomate*
tuna	*atún*
turkey	*pavo*

EATING OUT

smoking allowed	*se permite fumar*
no smoking	*se prohibe fumar*
menu	*la carta*
fork	*tenedor*
knife	*cuchillo*
spoon	*cuchara*
napkin	*servilleta*
glass of wine	*copa*
glass of beer	*caña*
water (mineral)	*agua (mineral)*
still/sparkling	*sin gas/con gas*
coffee (with milk)	*café (con leche)*
May I have the bill?	*La cuenta, por favor*
Do you take credit cards?	*¿Aceptan tarjetas de crédito?*
cakes	*pasteles*
small snacks	*pinchos*
sandwiches	*bocadillos*
set dishes	*platos combinados*

SHOPPING

ATM/cash machine	*cajero*
I want to buy…	*quiero comprar…*
I'm just looking	*sólo estoy mirando*
belt	*cinturón*
blouse	*blusa*
dress	*vestido*
shirt	*camisa*
shoes	*zapatas*
skirt	*falda*
tie	*corbata*
small	*pequeño*
medium	*mediano*
large	*grande*
cotton	*algodón*
silk	*seda*
wool	*lana*

NEED TO KNOW LANGUAGE

Timeline

From 3000BC–AD1500 the island was inhabited by Cro-Magnon and Mediterranean-type Stone Age people, who wore skins, kept livestock, grew cereals and had no written language. These aboriginal cavemen became known as the Guanches. According to accounts from early invaders, they were exceptionally tall and fair haired, and lived in caves carved out of the rock.

1340–42 Portuguese and Spanish send expeditions from Mallorca.

1405 The Norman Jean de Bethencourt fails in his attempt to conquer Gran Canaria for the Spanish throne.

1478 Juan Rejón founds the city of Real de las Palmas and begins subduing the island. The aboriginal people are led by two kings: Tenesor Semidan, who rules the west from his base at Gáldar, and Doramas, chief of the east, who rules from Telde. Rejón wins the first battle.

1479 Under the Treaty of Alcáçovas Portugal renounces its claims to the Canary Islands.

1481–82 King Doramas is killed at Montana de Arucas. King Tenesor Semidan is captured and taken to Spain where he then joins the Spanish cause.

1483 The Siege of Ansite ends with the surrender of most Canarians; this is the end of aboriginal resistance.

1492 Christopher Columbus stops in Las Palmas on his first voyage to the New World.

1496–c1525 Intensive colonization by Spaniards, Portuguese and Italians. Portuguese bring knowledge of the sugar cane industry from Madeira, which leads to growing prosperity for Gran Canaria from trade with the New World and the cultivation of sugar cane.

From left: Guanche caves at Cenobio de Valerón; Christopher Columbus monument in Las Palmas; sugar cane; restored Spanish galleon, Puerto Rico; the developed hillsides above Puerto Rico

18th–19th century The sugar trade collapses and the island's main exports become wine and cochineal.

1820 Las Palmas becomes the capital of Gran Canaria.

1852 The Canaries are declared a free trade zone in an effort to boost the islands' economy.

1927 Canary Islands are divided into two provinces; poverty results in emigration to Latin America.

1936 General Franco visits Gran Canaria and launches the military coup that begins the Spanish Civil War.

1950s Canarians demand home rule.

1960–70s Plans to develop the south for tourism begin.

1975–78 Franco dies and Spain becomes a constitutional monarchy under King Juan Carlos I.

1983 Spanish devolution leads to greater autonomy for the islands.

1986 Canary Islands become full members of the European Community as part of Spain.

2007 Severe forest fires burn out of control and destroy vast parts of the central landscape.

THE NAME

The first mention of the name 'Canaria' was by the Roman historian Pliny the Elder (AD23–79). He called the archipelago 'the Fortunate Isles' and named the main island Canaria, possibly because of the dogs (*canes* in Latin) that were found living there and which are still portrayed on the coat of arms of the Canary Islands.

BENITO PÉREZ GALDÓS

Pérez Galdós (1843–920), the 'Charles Dickens of Spain', was the youngest child in a family of 10, born to an army officer and his wife in Calle Cano 6 in the Triana district of Las Palmas (now a museum). He studied as a lawyer in Madrid before becoming a novelist and playwright. The island is extremely proud of Pérez Galdós, although he lived his adult life on the Spanish mainland.

Index

TWINPACK
Gran Canaria

WRITTEN BY Jackie Staddon and Hilary Weston
VERIFIED BY Penny Phenix and Jackie Staddon
COVER DESIGN AND DESIGN WORK Jacqueline Bailey
INDEXER Marie Lorimer
IMAGE RETOUCHING AND REPRO Sarah Montgomery, Michael Moody and James Tims
PROJECT EDITOR Stephanie Smith
SERIES EDITOR Cathy Harrison

© **AA MEDIA LIMITED 2010**

Colour separation by AA Digital Department
Printed and bound by Leo Paper Products, China

A CIP catalogue record for this book is available from the British Library.

ISBN 978-0-7495-6151-2

Published by AA Publishing, a trading name of AA Media Limited, whose registered office is Fanum House, Basing View, Basingstoke, Hampshire RG21 4EA. Registered number 06112600.

Front cover image: AA/C Sawyer
Back cover images: (i) AA/C Sawyer; (ii) AA/C Sawyer; (iii) AA/P Bennett; (iv) AA/P Bennett

A03639
Maps in this title produced from mapping © KOMPASS GmbH, A-6063 Rum, Innsbruck

The Automobile Association would like to thank the following photographers, companies and picture libraries for their assistance in the preparation of this book.

Abbreviations for the pictures credits are as follows – (t) top; (b) bottom; (c) centre; (l) left; (r) right; (AA) AA World Travel Library.

1 AA/J Tims; 2–18 top panel AA/P Bennett; 4 AA/P Bennett; 5 AA/J Tims; 6tl Courtesy of the Centro Atlantico de Arte Moderno (CAAM); 6tc AA/P Bennett; 6tr AA/P Bennett; 6bl AA/C Sawyer; 6bc AA/J Wyand; 6br AA/C Sawyer; 7tl AA/ S Day; 7tc AA/M Chaplow; 7tr AA/C Sawyer; 7bl AA/P Bennett; 7bc AA/A Mockford & N Bonetti; 7br AA/P Bennett; 10t AA/J Tims; 10c(i) AA/C Sawyer; 10c(ii) AA/ M Chaplow; 10b AA/J Tims; 11t(i) Photodisc; 11t(ii) AA/C Sawyer; 11c(i) AA/ C Sawyer; 11c(ii) AA/C Sawyer; 11b AA/P Bennett; 12t AA/C Sawyer; 12c(i) AA/ J Tims; 12c(ii) AA/P Bennett; 12b AA/P Bennett; 13t(i) Brand X Pics; 13t(ii) AA/ C Sawyer; 13c(i) AA/P Bennett; 13c(ii) AA/M Jourdan; 13b AA/J Wyand; 14t AA/ M Langford; 14c(i) AA/M Jourdan; 14c(ii) AA/C Sawyer; 14b AA/A Molyneux; 16t AA/C Sawyer; 16c(i) AA/J Tims; 16c(ii) Photodisc; 16b AA/P Bennett; 17t AA/ C Sawyer; 17c(i) AA/C Sawyer; 17c(ii) AA/C Sawyer; 17b AA/P Bennett; 18t AA/ P Bennett; 18c(i) AA/C Sawyer; 18c(ii) AA/C Sawyer; 18b AA/J Tims; 19t AA/ C Sawyer; 19c(i) AA/C Sawyer; 19c(ii) AA/P Bennett; 19b AA/J Tims; 20 AA/ P Bennett; 24 AA/C Sawyer; 24/25 AA/J Tims; 25 AA/P Bennett; 26l AA/C Sawyer; 26c AA/P Bennett; 26r AA/P Bennett; 27l AA/P Bennett; 27r AA/P Bennett; 28l AA/P Bennett; 28r AA/P Bennett; 29l AA/J Tims; 29r AA/C Sawyer; 30l AA/ P Bennett; 30tr AA/C Sawyer; 30br AA/P Bennett; 31t AA/C Sawyer; 31bl AA/ P Bennett; 31br AA/J Tims; 32–34 top panel AA/P Bennett; 32l AA/J Tims; 32r Courtesy of the Centro Atlantico de Arte Moderno (CAAM); 33l AA/C Sawyer; 33r Courtesy of the Museo Néstor; 34l AA/P Bennett; 34r AA/P Bennett; 35 AA/ C Sawyer; 36 AA/C Sawyer; 37–39 top panel AA/C Sawyer; 40–41 top panel AA/ J Tims; 42–44 top panel AA/C Sawyer; 45 AA/C Sawyer; 48l AA/C Sawyer; 48br AA/C Sawyer; 48/49 AA/C Sawyer; 49br AA/P Bennett; 49l AA/P Bennett; 50 Medio Images/ImageState; 51t AA/P Bennett; 51bl AA/P Bennett; 51br AA/ P Bennett; 52l AA/P Bennett; 52c AA/C Sawyer; 52r AA/J Tims; 53l AA/J Tims; 53r AA/J Tims; 54l AA/C Sawyer; 54c AA/C Sawyer; 54r AA/P Bennett; 55l AA/ C Sawyer; 55r AA/P Bennett; 56l AA/P Bennett; 56/57t AA/P Bennett; 56/57b AA/C Sawyer; 57br AA/P Bennett; 58–60 top panel AA/J Tims; 58l AA/ J Tims; 58r AA/J Tims; 59l AA/J Tims; 59r AA/J Tims; 60l AA/C Sawyer; 60r AA/ J Tims; 61l AA/J Tims; 61r AA/C Sawyer; 62 AA/P Bennett; 63 AA/J Tims; 64–65 top panel AA/C Sawyer; 66–67 top panel AA/J Tims; 68–70 top panel AA/C Sawyer; 71 AA/C Sawyer; 74l AA/J Tims; 74r AA/J Tims; 75l AA/J Tims; 75c AA/J Tims; 75r AA/P Bennett; 76l AA/C Sawyer; 76r AA/C Sawyer; 77t AA/ J Tims; 77b AA/P Bennett; 78l AA/J Tims; 78r AA/J Tims; 79l AA/P Bennett; 79r AA/C Sawyer; 80l AA/P Bennett; 80c AA/P Bennett; 80r AA/C Sawyer; 81l AA/ J Tims; 81r AA/J Tims; 82 AA/J Tims; 83–84 top panel AA/C Sawyer; 83l Chris Howes/Wild Places Photography/Alamy; 83r AA/P Bennett; 84l AA/P Bennett; 84r AA/J Tims; 85 AA/J Tims; 86 AA/C Sawyer; 87 AA/P Bennett; 90 AA/J Tims; 91t AA/J Tims; 91b AA/J Tims; 92l AA/P Bennett; 92c AA/P Bennett; 92r AA/ P Bennett; 93l AA/J Tims; 93r AA/J Tims; 94 AA/P Bennett; 94/95t AA/J Tims; 94/95b AA/C Sawyer; 95 AA/J Tims; 96 AA/C Sawyer; 97t AA/C Sawyer; 97b AA/ P Bennett; 98–101 top panel AA/C Sawyer; 98l AA/P Bennett; 98r AA/P Bennett; 99l AA/J Tims; 99r AA/J Tims; 100l AA/C Sawyer; 100r AA/C Sawyer; 101l AA/ J Tims; 101r Eddie Gerald/Alamy; 102 AA/P Bennett; 103 AA/J Tims; 104t AA/ C Sawyer; 104b AA/J Tims; 105–106 top panel AA/C Sawyer; 107 AA/J Tims; 108–112 top panel AA/C Sawyer; 108t(i) AA/J Tims; 108t(ii) AA/J Tims; 108c AA/ J Tims; 108b AA/J Tims; 109 AA/J Tims; 110–125 top panel AA/C Sawyer; 117 AA/P Bennett; 120 MRI Bankers Guide to Foreign Currency, Houston, USA; 124l AA/P Bennett; 124c AA/P Bennett; 124r AA/J Tims; 125l AA/J Tims; 125r AA/J Tims.

Every effort has been made to trace the copyright holders, and we apologise in advance for any accidental errors. We would be happy to apply any corrections in the following edition of this publication.